THE

ROOTS OF WAR
AND DOMINATION

Fred Burks
who has been exploring
these roots and their
connections also for a
long-time — Blessings

Ralph Metzner

ALSO BY RALPH METZNER

The Expansion of Consiousness (2008)

Sacred Vine of Spirits – Ayahuasca (2006)

Sacred Mushroom of Visions – Teonanácatl (2005)

Green Psychology: Transforming our Relationship to the Earth (1999)

The Unfolding Self: Varieties of Transformative Experience (1998)

The Well of Remembrance: Earth Wisdom Myths of Northern Europe (1994)

Through the Gateway of the Heart: Accounts of Experiences with MDMA and other Empathogenic Substances (1985)

Know Your Type: Maps of Identity (1979)

Maps of Consciousness: I Ching, Tantra, Tarot, Alchemy, Astrology, Actualism (1971)

The Ecstatic Adventure (1968)

The Psychedelic Experience: A Manual Based on the Tibetan Book of the Dead (1964: with Timothy Leary and Richard Alpert)

THE

ROOTS OF WAR

AND DOMINATION

by
Ralph Metzner

Green Earth Foundation
& REGENT PRESS

ISBN 13: 978-1-58790-150-8
ISBN 10: 1-58790-150-1
Library of Congress Control Number: 2008923032

Published by
REGENT PRESS
www.regentpress.net

for

GREEN EARTH FOUNDATION
www.greenearthfound.org

Manufactured in the U.S.A.
REGENT PRESS
2747 Regent Street
Berkeley, CA 94705
e-mail: regentpress@mindspring..com

Printed on 30% post-consumer recycled fiber,
archival [acid free] paper

Acknowledgements

This book is the second in a series of six short books – with the general title *The Ecology of Consciousness* – which are being produced and published by the Green Earth Foundation, in collaboration with Regent Press. My heartfelt gratitude and deep appreciation goes to: (1) the Board of Directors of the Green Earth Foundation, for their moral and material support on this writing and publishing project, as well as the Alchemical Divination training; (2) Michael Ziegler and Leigh Marz, and to Sophia Bowart and Peggy Hitchcock, for financial support; (3) Mark Weiman of Regent Press, for arriving at just the right time to handle the logistics of publishing and distribution; (4) my assistant Cynthia Smith for her meticulous attention to the design and lay-out of the book; and, last but not least, to my wife Cathy and daughter Sophia, for co-creating and maintaining a harmonious household, in which this creative writing, publishing and teaching work can grow and flourish.

Sonoma, California
January 2008

Note:

It was my original intention to combine this essay on the *Roots of War and Domination*, with an earlier essay of mine, called *Pride, Prejudice and Paranoia – Dismantling the Ideology of Domination* (published in *World Futures*, 1998). It is my aim however, to keep each of the books in this series to under 100 pages. Readers who would like to read the earlier essay, in which I compare five different forms of domination (nationalism, racism, sexism, classism and the humanist domination of nature), may do so by going to the Green Earth Foundation website (http://greenearthfound.org/write/pride.html).

Contents

Author's Preface

My life-long almost obsessive interest in the causes of war and how to end it is rooted, not surprisingly, in my personal history. I feel I owe it to the reader to explain how I came to have a peculiar fascination for this most ancient, deep-seated and tragic feature of human life. I was born in 1936 in Germany and lived there with my family, until 1947, after which my two brothers and I emigrated to Britain, with my mother. My father was German and my mother Scottish, so during the Second World War, my father's people and my mother's people were busy trying to annihilate one another. We lived in Berlin, where my father was the director of a successful family publishing business. When the allied bombing raids started, and we heard the wailing air-raid sirens, always at night, we would be hustled down to the basement in our pajamas, with blankets and hot chocolate, listening to the radio news announcer, until the ending siren sounded. Our house did not get a bomb hit, and from the child's point of view, the war did not much affect our safe bourgeois existence – at least, not until the end. In early 1945, our family received the news that my father's younger brother, who was a fighter pilot in the *Luftwaffe*, was shot down on the Eastern front. His death was an event that was never mentioned, veiled by a strange aura of incomprehension and silent sorrow.

Because of the circumstances of my childhood, I was fortunate to learn an early lesson in the delusional aspects of war-time propaganda. In Berlin during World War II, the public atmosphere of school and media was filled with talk of "the

English are our enemies," "we're going to drive them into the sea," and the like; while in the private sphere of our family and friends, there was, of course, no such conversation. There were discussions about war, and the terrible news of battles and deaths. They were accepted by the child as something impersonal that just happened, similarly to discussions about really bad weather, happening someplace else and not here.

When, during adolescence, I lived in a boarding school in the North of Scotland, I saw that to the English children, the Germans, myself included, were the "enemy" or "bad guys." I was subject to the arrogant teasing and verbal bullying of children under the sway of an "enemy" image. From these experiences, my child's mind thus absorbed the fact that "enemies" don't actually exist – they are subjectively determined projected images. We label or categorize another being an "enemy" to serve as a target for our projected hatred and hostility. Later, as a young adult, I was grateful to my parents for inadvertently providing me with this early opportunity for learning about the subjectivity and relativity of "enemies." Later still, I came to appreciate how these growth experiences of my childhood were a fateful and graceful consequence of my parents' shared passion for international peacemaking.

In the Spring of 1945, as the allied forces poured into Germany from the West, and the Russians from the East, somber incomprehensible rumors of Russian soldiers raping women and girls, from seven to seventy, began to be whispered among the adults. I did not know what "raping" meant, but I understood the threat of violence implicit in the German word for it – *Vergewaltigung*. It became imperative to go West, toward the allied armies, said to be less animalistic, and less bent on revenge than the Russians, who had suffered immense losses at the hands of the German military forces. My mother travelled by train, with the three children, toward Hamburg, where we had relatives, and later to a children's home in Schleswig-Holstein for safety. My father had been drafted into a military reserve unit and sent to Paris in the occupation army, because of his French language skills. As the Germans retreated from France, he, like many at that time, struggled to extricate himself from the army and avoid being executed for desertion.

My strongest and most troubling memory from this time comes from a train-ride, probably on the exit journey to the West, out of Berlin. We were in a full train compartment with other adult passengers. It must have been late in the war, since there was talk among some of the men of how the war was going, and what would happen afterwards, if "we" (Germany) lost the war. A man sitting in one corner, who had been silent, suddenly spoke up and said, looking at the man who had spoken of defeat, *Wie meinen Sie das?* ("How do you mean that?") The tone of his voice sent a steel-cold, prickly sensation up the back of my neck, and a heavy atmosphere of fear settled into the compartment, ending all discussion. The eight-year old boy understood only much later why, in the context of a fascist dictatorship, where talk of defeat was considered traitorous, that seemingly innocuous question was imbued with such menace. The feeling of nameless terror however, was unmistakable.

As the nation of Germany collapsed, we were ferried by our relatives out of Hamburg, to escape the bombing raids, further into the country. I recall throngs of hundreds trying to board a crowded train with all their luggage. Once we even travelled some distance in a freight train carriage, uncovered, filled with coal dust. In the Children's Home by the seaside, there was relative peace, though we could still hear the English bombers droning across the night sky. There was however, near-starvation, as the overweight matron and her assistants, hogged much of the meager food rations, depriving their charges of minimal nutrition. I remember a gnawing hunger so intense, that I once picked up from the street an old bread crust, which tasted of dog piss.

I remember all four of us (my brothers and I and our mother) living, eating, cooking and sleeping, in one upstairs room rented out to us by a local farmer. Long lines of Russian prisoners of war were marched through the streets by German guards, to go to some kind of work-camp. One time, an SS officer came to the door, asking questions. His uniform was completely black, from the cap to the long jack-boots; on his black helmet were the skull and cross-bones insignia of the *Todesstaffel.* Then, after we were in that village for a couple of months perhaps, the war ended, and the British army liberated the prisoner of war camp. Now the violence and threat came from the other side, as the freed Russians rampaged through the villages and farms, slaughtering sheep in the field for food, daring the farmer to stop them. Unpredictable violence or the threat of it pervaded the atmosphere of the place. Eventually my mother, because she was English born, obtained a job with the British occupation forces, and life returned to some semblance of normalcy. All shops were more or less empty, and I remember finding it hard to believe my mother, who stated that "normal" meant, and would again mean, that the shops were full of things to buy – like clothes, and school supplies, and fresh foods, the essentials of a child's life.

Then, in 1947, we were given permission to sail to Scotland, to live with my mother's relatives at first, and in boarding schools, later. And on this voyage, the 11-year old boy learned another profound, decisive lesson about the meaning of war (although I wouldn't have thought about it that way till much later). The childish image of war that I had somehow absorbed from the family and other adults, was that it was like some kind of game or competition, in which there were "winners" and "losers " I felt I had experienced and understood what it was for a country, or nation, to "lose the war" – it meant destroyed buildings, random violence, occupying armies with strange languages, food rationing and other deprivations, such as shortage of clothing. I somehow thought that in the country that "won the war," things would be different, children and other people would be "better off." But when we arrived in England and Scotland, I saw there were also destroyed buildings, and serious deprivations and shortages. I remember thinking, in my childish way, "what a strange game, where the winners are just as badly off as the losers." What then, was the point of all this?

The futility of the mutual destruction and loss in wars, and the relativity and subjectivity of enemies – these observations from my childhood constituted a troubling set of questions that have haunted me all my life. Later learning and experience have only deepened and confirmed the impression I gained then, and strengthened the motivation to try to understand the underlying causes of war and help alleviate its horrible consequences. In my adolescence I used to imagine that I would become a diplomat, or work for some international agency that promoted cross-cultural understanding. My mother worked for many years for UNESCO, travelling around the world to many different places, and I thought I could somehow follow in her footsteps. My father's business in Germany was less attractive to me as a career choice, though I admired his *francophile, anglophile* and generally transnational attitudes and values.

Much later in my life, when I worked as a psychologist and shamanic guide with processes of tracking ancestral and karmic lines of fate, I came to see how the soul's choice of a family in which to be conceived and born can be a prefiguring of the mission or vision for that life. I observed that when parents come from radically different or antagonistic religions, ethnicity, or nationality – the bridging and healing of such differences usually turns out to be an important aspect of that individual's life-path vision. Innumerable stories from literature and film carry the message that a couple from warring or feuding tribes who love one another and found a family, are committed peacemakers, even when their project is tragically aborted, as in the story of *Romeo and Juliet.*

My parents came from very different worlds: my father was a German middle-class professional with a doctorate in political science, my mother was from a working-class background in Scotland, without a college education, who knew no German. They met, fell in love and married while they both were working at the League of Nations in Geneva. Their shared commitment and passion for building bridges across national boundaries have been guiding values for my life, symbolically resonant with my life's work of building bridges of understanding between different worlds of consciousness and culture.

***

I would therefore like to dedicate this work to my parents, and to the peacemakers in every tribe and nation and world. They are indeed the Children of God.

The Roots of War and Domination

How did domination and violence become part of human nature? Or, if it is not part of human nature, how did it become such a prominent feature of civilization? As the world political situation descends once again into a maelstrom of war and destruction, thoughtful people everywhere are asking themselves and each other these questions, even as activists and diplomats struggle to find means to end the mayhem. Media images crowd the mind: the grief-struck mother whose house has been bombed and whose children killed, asks "why – what did we do to them?" The military leader who ordered the high-tech precision bombing raids on civilian settlements, says "we bombed because we had to – we had no choice." Of course, reasons are always given, there are "strategic purposes," the "defense of vital interests," the "nation's security," "securing our borders," "the other side started it."

For everyone of these reasons, there are always sober, reasonable voices who point out these purposes and interests could perhaps better be served by non-violent means, and that the path of violence usually (always?) ends up doing more harm than good to those very interests. There is a sense of some compulsion, addictive almost, some other hidden element we can't quite discern that keeps pushing humanity into homicidal and suicidal madness. What is that hidden dynamic, that seemingly demonic obsession? Where does it come from? What does it mean? Can we ever overcome it? I wish to look at some esoteric legends and speculative histories for possible clues to this most agonizing dilemma. Before looking at the marginal or alternative theories, let us review those writings that locate the roots of war and violence in child development of the individual, in historical patterns of tribal competition, and in the vagaries of human evolution.

Psychological Roots of Violence in Child Development

At the most basic level of individual development, most people would agree that violence and domination, like all other forms of behavior, are learned by imitation. It is widely accepted from psychological studies of violent criminals that violence is learned behavior. Adults who abuse others, including their own children, are likely to have been abused themselves, and/or witnessed abuse in childhood. The cause of violence, in other words, is prior violence. Furthermore, ample research demonstrates that physical punishment only amplifies the disposition to further violence.

Similar trends can be observed at the level of community and society: wars lead to further wars, whether between street gangs, tribes or nation states. It's almost as if violence and domination were a kind of contagious virus that infects certain human lineages. This dominator virus (or *meme*, as some would call it)[1] is expressed in families as possessiveness and abusive controlling behavior; or in infected communities through violent crime and abuse toward domestics, minorities, out-groups and animals. The contagion is magnified in society by entertainment media saturated with images and stories that glamorize violence as heroic, and that desensitize the individual to the terrible human costs and consequences of violence, normalizing it and blunting our capacity for empathy. In the heavily militarized societies of modern times, conditions favor the spread of violence from the military to the civilian sectors: statistical studies have shown that the rate of violent crime in a society goes up in war time.

In this chicken-and-egg kind of complex causal situation, we can ask, how and where does the initial impulse to violence, arise?

What conditions create the susceptibility to being infected by the dominator virus?

Sibling Rivalry and Competition

Psychologists studying child development have identified one possible source in sibling rivalry, the competition between brothers and sisters for the attention and approval of the parents and other adults, especially when there is a perceived scarcity of loving connection. The competitive attitude may be maintained into adulthood and carried over into personal and work relationships with peers. The analogy then at the societal level is the theory that wars arise in competition over access to scarce resources, such as land or energy – a view which we will discuss further below.

In the family crucible of child development, the experiences of sibling rivalry and violent abuse may be internalized: the person may develop a dual self-image – a good and bad self, or "top dog" and "under dog," as Fritz Perls, the founder of Gestalt therapy, called this constellation. Religious mythology as well as folk tales and fairy tales are filled with stories of rival brothers and sisters, playing out the many variations of this theme. In more extreme situations of childhood violence, there may be the development of multiple part-self fragments, some violent and dominant, some fearful victims, some detached and alienated. Then, in adulthood, these internalized images of "opponent" and "rival" are projected outward, adding excess charges of rage, hatred and fear into interpersonal relations.

The Shadow Complex

One of the most provocative of C.G. Jung's many contributions to psychology in the 20th century, is his concept of the shadow, – a complex of unacceptable thoughts, feelings and images, that seem to work against our own better interests, countering our higher values, a kind of "enemy within." This shadow complex may appear symbolically in a dream of a monster; or it may be projected outward on our fellow humans, whom we then regard as an "enemy," or "evil." Jung argued that for psychological health or wholeness, we need to integrate this shadow complex, reconcile with this inner enemy. If we don't integrate these hidden parts of the psyche we are liable to be surprised by its sudden and violent eruptions in altered states of rage, panic and violence.

In my book *The Unfolding Self* (Metzner, 1998) I discuss this key integrative and healing process, as it may manifest in the course of psychotherapy or other growth processes, in the chapter on "Reconciling with the Inner Enemy." One of the central insights of depth psychology is that there are two main types of defenses that we use to avoid confronting the negative, anxiety-provoking thought-feeling impulses within ourselves; and they require different strategies to bring about integration and reconciliation. The defense of repression, dissociation or denial requires that unconscious material be brought to here-now awareness, so it can be dealt with.

The defense of projection, in which some *other* is blamed and seen as the enemy, or the "evil-doer," or the "bad guy," is much trickier to work with, since it requires the withdrawing of the blame-judgement projections, and accepting one's own negativity.

The process is trickier because there is almost always a seed of truth in projections, some hook on which to hang the projected image. As long as the processes of shadow projection keep us externally focused, it is all too easy for intra-psychic conflict to erupt into interpersonal or inter-group enmity and conflict. In either case the processes of healing and reconciliation require skillful analytic detective work as well as empathy, both for others and for oneself.

The shadow metaphor also applies at the level of collective consciousness, where we are dealing with mass-mind images. These are complexes of unconscious personal material combined with the consciously propagated enemy images or memes of religion and politics. The Christian devil, it could be said, is such a symbolic mass-mind enemy image that acquired a certain autonomy and power over human beings, due to its being invested with belief over many centuries by many millions of the Christian faithful.

Fanatical and unscrupulous group leaders activate mass-mind shadow images self-hate and shame, originating in infancy or childhood. When a dualistic hate-shame complex is activated, it is projected outward and a splitting occurs: the leader of the party, or the *Volk*, or the nation, is said to be "good," and the designated external enemy or internal scapegoat is designated "bad" or "evil." The chosen scapegoated individuals (which could be Jews, terrorists, Muslims, women, blacks) are then beaten down and humiliated, the way the child-self was beaten down and humiliated. Or, if the individual has identified more with the underdog or scapegoat, victim roles may be sought out in various situations.

In my own personal history, I was fortunate to acquire an early understanding of the delusional aspects of war-time propaganda and the subjectivity of enemy-making. A moment's reflection will show that "shadows" and "enemies" don't actually exist. We may say they have a kind of virtual reality, the power to affect our behavior in the world through shaping our beliefs and perceptions.

Child Abuse and Attachment Disorders in Infancy

In the work of Lloyd DeMause and his psychohistory colleagues, who bring psychoanalytic insights to scholarly studies of historical events and processes, the connections between individual trauma and public violence has been made explicit. Their work, published in the *Journal of Psychohistory* (www. psychohistory.com) as well as several major books by DeMause, presents an immense body of historical and anthropological documentation on the prevalence of child abuse, neglect and abandonment, in all periods of history and all cultures up to and including the present. The findings on the amount of violent child abuse are so staggering as to provoke incredulity and denial at first glance, yet the conclusions and implications are inescapable.[2] Childhood, in most eras of the past and most parts of the world even today, is rife with psychic dramas of rage, sacrifice and humiliation, which are later re-enacted on the world stage, in wars and violent revolutions, by leaders carrying the projections of their followers.

An example of the way individual trauma can be translated on to the world historical stage is the way Adolf Hitler, who was himself repeatedly brutally beaten and humiliated as a child by his father, used the image of the *Dolchstoss*, the "dagger in the back," to symbolize the enormously burdensome and humiliating reparations that Germany was forced to pay by the winners in WW I. This image then activated feelings of vengefulness and hatred in ordinary Germans, feelings that they knew from their own childhood experiences of abuse and injustice. DeMause concludes that wars are a kind of self-sacrificial blood-letting ritual that nations are drawn into by leaders with unassimilated childhood trauma. Such mass blood-letting rituals are designed to appease internalized authoritarian voices that demand dependence, sacrifice and obedience.

It is difficult to do justice, in brief, to the breadth and depth of DeMause's work over the past thirty years: it covers not only the history and evolution of child-rearing modes and how that affects the mass psychology underlying war, but also the devastating effects of child abuse on the creation of the dissociated personality systems of killers and torturers, whether in war or in peacetime. In an essay on the "The Psychology and Neurobiology of Violence," (which is excerpted from his forthcoming book on *The Origins of War in Child Abuse*) DeMause reviews current research on the neurobiological aspects of the crucial attachment period of earliest infancy:

> In the past two decades over a hundred careful studies have shown that violence is the result of insecure/disorganized early attachments. Furthermore, in recent years major advances in neurobiological techniques have revealed how these early disordered attachments are embedded in the brain and are reenacted in later life in personal and social violence...

> The mind and therefore the emotional content of the brain are created in the first few years of life through the attachment bond between the infant and the primary caretaker...From the very beginning, the mother's emotionally expressive face and eyes are the most important objects in the infant's world and the infant's wide pupils evoke the

mother's gaze and increase her oxytocin, stimulating her attachment
and especially her empathy, as registered in her mirror neurons...

Even rhesus monkeys who are separated at birth from their mother's
gaze grow up fearful and violently attack other monkeys. Insecurely
attached children actually display nine times as much aggression as
their securely attached peers. Obviously the degree of infant-maternal
attachment crucially affects the amount of violence later acted out by
adults. (DeMause, 2007b).

It is now known that the most common response of the child
to chronic traumatic physical and sexual abuse and neglect is
not repression, in which fear-charged memories are supposedly
buried in a more primitive reservoir of the psyche to erupt only
in fantastic and disorganized form in dreams or psychosis – but
rather *dissociation*. Dissociation itself is the normal psycho-
neural function of disconnecting – the opposite of associative
connecting. The ability to focus or concentrate one's attention is
crucially dependent on the ability to dissociate from distracting
stimuli. In dissociative disorders however, or their extreme form
of multiple personality disorders, one or more ego-states are
separated into functional *alters*. Each of these *alters* has its own
stream of thoughts, memories, feelings, sensations and impulses,
with internal coherence and consistency, but separated by what is
called an "amnestic barrier" from one another.

To bring such dissociated ego-states and *alters* back
together requires difficult and time-consuming deep altered
state hypnotherapy. To compound the difficulty, individuals
with dissociative disorders, harboring rageful or persecutory
alters, may not seek treatment and may not even experience
any distress or manifest any disturbed behavior – until they
"switch" into a parallel *alter*. Unlike psychosis, which involves
a more or less complete disorganization and fragmentation of
identity, a dissociated identity disorder involves an organized

compartmentalization of separate functional identities, that may "switch" when triggered by certain stimuli, with total lack of awareness. As DeMause writes:

> *Alters* are the time bombs embedded in the right brain during childhood that are the sources of all later violence. Because they are dissociated modules, the adult can seem to be any personality mode, even passive and withdrawn, but when they act out the earlier hurts and fears and rages against a Bad Self victim, they can become a murderer or a terrorist or soldier massacring thousands without guilt. It is the dissociated aspect of social violence and war that allows so many psychologists to conclude that men like Goehring or Auschwitz guards or Bin Laden are 'perfectly normal,' since their left-brain personalities are well organized, not 'psychotic,' while their right-brain dissociated alter modules periodically take over and commit their violence. (DeMause, 2007b).

Birth Trauma

Tracking even further back in infancy to the perinatal ("around birth") period and the prenatal period, a very considerable body of research over the past twenty years has revealed that the birth process itself, especially under the sterile mechanized conditions of the standard obstetrical delivery room can leave profoundly traumatic imprints in the deepest layers of the psyche. Fortunately, in certain subcultures of the West, such practices are becoming ameliorated under the influence of progressive movements toward conscious, spiritually-centered birthing practices. The field of perinatal and prenatal psychology offers a rich set of convincing observations on the roots of aggression and violence in the experience of the birth trauma and the details of fetal existence.

Transpersonal psychiatric researcher Stanislav Grof, whose original theories were based on observations in LSD

psychotherapy and holotropic breathwork, has shown how the
fetus's experiences in the different stages of the birth process
functions as a kind of matrix (what he calls a *basic perinatal
matrix*), typically and spontaneously associated with a variety of
experiences from the collective unconscious portraying scenes of
terror and aggression.

In his book *The Psychology of the Future*, Grof describes these
collective manifestations of perinatal trauma:

> ...the reliving of birth in various forms of experiential psychotherapy
> involves not only concrete replay of the original emotions and
> sensations, but is typically associated with a variety of experiences
> from the collective unconscious portraying scenes of unimaginable
> violence. Among these are often powerful sequences depicting wars,
> revolutions, racial riots, concentration camps, totalitarianism, and
> genocide...The spontaneous emergence of this imagery during the
> reliving of birth is often associated with convincing insights concerning
> the perinatal origin of such extreme forms of human violence. (Grof,
> 2000, p. 302).

DeMause (2007) elaborates on this perinatal theme as well,
writing that he finds in his psychohistorical analyses of political
propaganda during the run-up period prior to a war, "that wars
are from their beginning experienced as direct repetition of the
birth struggle, begun when nations are 'smothered and unable to
draw a breath,' continuing until they can 'see the light at the end
of the tunnel' and even 'aborted' if ended too soon."

One of Hitler's favorite *memes*, that he used to inspire
ordinary Germans for his aggressive push eastward, was that
the German people needed a larger *Lebensraum* ("living space"),
which is a typical thought for the fetus struggling through the
constrictive conditions of the birth canal at term. The destructive
dropping of bombs is also associated with the birth process.
During the first Gulf war, Saddam Hussein was famously quoted
as promising that the American invaders would encounter the

"mother of all battles" and cartoons showed him pregnant with a bomb. Even the dropping of the nuclear bomb on Hiroshima was seen as a birthing ritual: The bomb was nicknamed "Little Boy" and dropped from the belly of a plane named after the pilot's mother. When it was dropped, General Groves cabled President Truman that "The baby was born."

On the mother's side of the birthing interaction, the mother's own birth and infancy trauma can be activated by the intense emotional and physical arousal of the birthing process, triggering the mother into dissociated traumatized ego-states.[3] DeMause writes:

> The parents of the caretaker are still present as "ghosts in the nursery" when the child is born, in the form of dissociated persecutory alters (alternative personalities) – internal objects and voices that repeat the traumas and fears the caretaker experienced as a child, since 'the hurtful parent was once a hurt child'...When the alter is activated, the mother experiences herself as the good, persecuted mother while the baby is seen as primarily bad, utterly persecuting and a justifiable object of hatred. The helpless, vulnerable child experiences this reenactment of maternal fear and hatred as ending in abandonment and death." (DeMause, Lloyd., 2007a).

The work of the psychohistory scholars in disentangling the complex causal web between dissociative reactions to trauma during birth and infancy in the individual, and the fear and hate projections propagated through the mass-mind before and during wars, is ongoing and of great subtlety and significance. It can be hoped that the progressive movements advocating more conscious birthing practices that are centered in a respectful spiritual attitude towards the child being born, as well as the parents, will contribute toward the gradual evolution of human adults less prone to violence and less susceptible to the enemy-making propaganda of power-hungry leaders. DeMause himself has stated that the decision by mothers (and increasingly fathers as well) to treat the birth and infancy of their children with more conscious caring and respect than they themselves were treated as children, may be one of the key levers of evolutionary progress.

***

In considering the possible personal developmental origins of violence, terror and war, I was always still left with a nagging sense of incompleteness, a sense perhaps of deeper forces at work. Why is it that some cultures develop and propagate the habits of domination in the family and the scape-goating of out-groups, whereas other cultures do not? Are there deeper ancestral, historical and prehistorical forces at work here, that have driven tribes and states to resort to violence and war? This is the question I wish to address next.

Historical and Prehistorical Roots in Tribal Competition

No one can deny that the collective human manifestations of war and violence have horrifyingly long historical and pre-historical antecedents in the age-old, long-continuing struggles between tribes and societies for territory and economic survival. Many believe that all war is basically fought over resources: in historical times at first over land and animals; later, the extraction of valuable minerals and metals; still later, in the petroleum age, the biosphere's stored carbon deposits. Contemporary indications are that water may turn out to be the most bitterly fought over resource in this era of global fever-heat and climate-change.

The cut-throat competition of the 'haves' and the 'have-nots' seems to be a deeply ingrained factor in the consciousness of the human race. Just how deeply ingrained is a question of intense debate among anthropologists, historians and archaeologists. Can we transform territorial and economic competition into peaceful and cooperative co-existence? Have we ever? Is there any evidence that peaceful societies have ever existed, which would give us hope that it can be done?

Here the work of archaeologist Marija Gimbutas on the matricentric, peaceful, goddess-worshipping cultures of Old Europe, in the 8th to 6th millennia BCE, is of great importance (Gimbutas, 1991). Although her work is controversial because it goes far beyond the accepted academic paradigms in prehistory and archaeology, I am among those who find the massive accumulation of detailed evidence in her work to be convincing in a revelatory way. Around the 5th millennium BCE, the people she calls *Kurgans*, with their sky and warrior gods, their horses, chariots and weapons, started emigrating from their homeland in

Central Asia, perhaps in reaction to spreading drought conditions (for which there is independent evidence). Gimbutas' work shows, convincingly to my mind, that the Kurgan peoples' practice of invading the rich farming communities along river valleys and taking what they wanted by force of arms, was not a form of culture that could have evolved naturally out of those peaceful, artistic cultures of Old Europe. It was imposed by violence and war at first, and later by forced assimilation and intermarriage.

The historical outcome of these millennia-long transformations were hybrid cultures, in which there was a ruling class or caste of patriarchal warrior chiefs and kings, and a subordinate class of farmers and other workers. Some scholars have suggested that the ancient Indian civilization, with its rigid hereditary caste structure, was similarly a product of an over layering of dominant Aryans over the indigenous Dravidians.

In my book *The Well of Remembrance* (Metzner, 1994) I show how hybrid mythologies wove together the histories and religious cosmologies of the two kinds of cultures in Europe. In Nordic-Germanic mythology as related in *The Edda*, the deities of the Old Europeans, called *Vanir*, were all associated with the land, fertility, peace and wealth, including mineral wealth. The sky and warrior deities, called *Aesir*, were originally the protector gods of the nomadic herders, highly dependent on sun and weather changes. *The Edda* poems say that war came to mankind by extension from the competitive feuding between the Aesir and Vanir deities. These myths are religious stories that tell the histories of the peoples involved. The invaders and conquerors tell their justification stories – "they stole from us," "they started the fighting," "our supreme god told us do this." The conquered also tell their stories – of resistance and retaliation; but also of peacemaking and reconciliation rituals – like the Mysteries of Eleusis, and the story of the Mead of Inspiration. We shall return below to the hidden and eerie connections between religions and war.

Capitalism, Colonialism and Militarism

Certainly it is not difficult to see how the attitude of conquering robbers and pirates, who take the resources they want from militarily less powerful populations, using violence or the threat of violence, can be seen in the history of colonialism, with its "conquistadors," and industrial capitalism, with its "robber barons" and "titans of industry." The pernicious parallels between a war-based economy and criminal gangsterism have rarely been pointed out as forcefully and as bluntly as by the highly decorated Marine Corps general Smedley D. Butler, in his book *War is a Racket*:

> I spent thirty-three years and four months in active military service as a member of this country's most agile military force, the Marine Corps…And during that period, I spent most of my time being a high-class muscle-man for Big Business, for Wall Street and the Bankers…War is a racket. It always has been. It is possibly the oldest, easily the most profitable, surely the most vicious…It is the only one in which the profits are reckoned in dollars and the losses in lives (Butler, 1935).

The insidious connection between large business corporations and an aggressive war-based economy can also be seen in the domineering financial and market manipulations of multinational corporations in our own time. Industrial corporations were originally created as legal mechanisms to organize and facilitate the production and distribution of goods and services in an economy. But they suffer from an inherent design flaw, namely that the explicit and primary purpose of their operations is the continuous generating of profit. The purpose of a business, we are told in textbooks, is to make money; whereas actually the purpose should be (and was, originally) the production of shoes, bread and other "goods," and the provision of services, such as transportation or construction.

The excessive and exclusive focus on the bottom line of profitability has turned the corporations into rogue machine monsters, hierarchical systems of organized taking, called "capital accumulation." These machine monsters have escaped the control of their makers, and are systematically, at ever increasing speed and intensity, exploiting and devouring all of the planet's biosphere elements. These biosphere elements were originally, in pre-industrial societies, kept as shared common wealth, or the "commons." Increasingly, over the past two or three centuries of the growth of capitalism, they have become "resources" to be turned into commodities for sale: they include land (especially fertile soil), water, forests, ocean fisheries, minerals and metals, carbon deposits and even the electro-magnetic spectrum, used for radio and other forms of communication. Most recently, in their relentless drive to find resources to exploit, giant chemical companies, such as Monsanto, have started to appropriate (by the patenting of genetic modifications) the genomes of plant species that have served as traditional food sources in countries such as India for millennia (Shiva, 2000).

The capitalist project of economic domination and exploitation of the biosphere is driving countless plant and animal species to irreversible extinction by habitat destruction, and pushing indigenous human populations into destitution.

From this perspective, tribal and national warfare is the inevitable accompaniment to the organized taking, or theft, of raw materials or resources. Indo-European cattle herders with superior weapons found that it was temptingly easy to enlarge their herds of cattle (the word "capital" is derived from the counting of heads of cattle), by raiding the herds of others and killing or enslaving their owners. English sailing ships exploring the Americas in search of gold, found a more easily profitable return on their backers' investments was to be had by resorting to piracy, by stealing from the Spanish who had already mined the gold with the slave labor of the Indians. European history, as told in textbooks, is a long and repetitive story of first, monarchies and later, nation states using military means to enlarge or consolidate their territories.

In our time, the pattern continues, as the industrial capitalist corporations, with their relentless drive for profitability, constantly scour the globe for cheaper raw materials, as well as markets for their products – backed up by the military force of an expanding empire striving for "full-spectrum" dominance. As Karl Marx and his successors pointed out, since capitalism is fixated on permanent growth, it tends naturally to develop in concert with imperialism and war (Magdoff, 1978).

Violence, war or the threat of war, usually accompany the taking of resources owned or protected by others – just as theft is usually armed robbery. But the use of force or violence has fateful consequences: wars of aggression lead to wars of defense. As Andrew Bard Schmookler pointed out in his book *The Parable of the Tribes* (Schmookler, 1984), if you have a group of tribes living peaceably, and only one of them starts to arm itself and threaten or attack another, all of them have to resort to arms to defend themselves. Wars of aggression, or even the threat of violence, lead inevitably to further wars, just as violence between gangs leads to further retaliatory violence, and violence in the family begets further violence in the next generation.

Even more insidiously, the making and improvement of weaponry and armaments becomes an ever-growing pre-occupation of the ruling elites. The technologies of killing require the growth of specialized knowledge, the diversion of wealth into the production of the sharper swords, the faster firearms, the more powerful bombs, and the ever greater influence and power of the military castes in society. It was Dwight Eisenhower, the general who became President, who warned Americans of the threat to a free society posed by the enormous growth and "unwarranted influence" of the military-industrial complex.

The mutuality of the relationship between capitalism and warfare was demonstrated both by the growth of the Nazi military machine in the 1930s (supported by both German and American corporations); and by the success of the armaments industry in lifting America out of the Depression. In our time, by far most profitable sector of the industrial economy is military and defense related, as the self-styled "superpower" rampages across the globe, selling more weaponry than all other countries combined (Blum, 2000).

However, the success and profitability of the military comes at a huge cost to society. In our time, in the United States, we have obscenely bloated military budgets, and a world-wide trade in arms that dwarfs the trade in all other products (with the possible exception of drugs), as declining portions of the society's wealth are used for infrastructure, education, and health care for the poor. Other countries fall victim to this imbalance as well: the Russian economy imploded under the weight of its excessive military-industrial bureaucracy. We have countries like North

Korea, where nuclear missile technology co-exists with mass starvation. On the other side of the equation – Germany and Japan, the defeated nations of WWII, which were forbidden to spend money on re-arming their military, made a much faster recovery in their economies after the war than other European nations.

There is a fateful connection between capitalism and militarism at the societal level, just as there is between addiction and violence at the local, tribal level. Force is needed to support the addiction. The relentless drive for profits and growth in the capitalist system is backed by military force; and military spending is the ready solution to capitalism's biggest weakness – overproduction. The military-industrial complex soaks up excess capital looking for investment, and provides consumption without limits, in a vicious cycle closely analogous to drug addiction. This malignant connection is made strikingly clear, in the comic-book format book *Addiction to Militarism* (Andreas, 2002).

The Military as Parasitical to Civil Society

It should be recognized clearly: to maintain a military system does not actually contribute to the productive wealth of a society. True, military-industrial corporations generate profits for their investors, soaking up enormous amounts of money; and they employ a certain number of people, both in the armed forces and the civilian sector. However, they don't contribute "goods and services" to the country's overall economy, its infrastructure, the well-being of its people, the uplifting of the poor, or the improvement of its natural environment; nor do they contribute to the diversity and vibrancy of cultural life. From an ecological perspective, the relationship of the military system to the larger socio-economic order is parasitical: resources are drained from the productive sectors of society to feed the growth of the military system, and the inequalities inherent in a capitalist society are exacerbated enormously.

In suggesting that the relation of the military war-system to the larger society is analogous to the relationship of a parasite to its host, I do not assume that it must necessarily be that way. Clearly it is a function of the budgetary priorities given to the military by the leaders of the society, and these in turn are determined by the growth needs of industrial capitalism. A purely defensive military capability could be integrated into a society in a balanced way, and there are evolutionary models for that: in ant colonies, the soldier ants and worker ants each contribute their function to the overall maintenance of the society. Federations and treaties can be used to reduce the threat of aggression and invasion by outsiders. On this analogy, the challenge for a mature human society would be to balance the expenditures on necessary defensive forces with expenditures on the environment, infrastructure, health care and other basic human needs.

The parasite analogy has been applied to the relation of global humanity to the planetary biosphere. Ecological thinkers, including James Lovelock, the inventor of the Gaia theory (Lovelock, 1991) have proposed that the linked problems of overpopulation and environmental degradation can be seen as symptoms of a planetary disease: like a parasitical infestation of the biosphere (Lovelock ironically labels it "disseminated primatemia"), human beings threaten the viability of numerous plant and animal species and the irreparable destruction of numerous habitats.

Not all parasite-host relationships end up with the death of one or the other. Evolution has countless models in which a parasitical relationship between species has been turned into a symbiotic mutuality. The global challenge, in this analogy, is for the human civilization, fractured and dysfunctional though it may be, instead of dominating and exploiting the biosphere, to become its stewards and preservers.

* * *

But why exactly do some societies evolve a market system based on the profit motive, traditionally known as "greed," rather than on meeting all human needs and Earth's needs first? Is it not possible to imagine that groups (or tribes, or nations) inhabiting a particular area, confronted with a situation of scarce resources, would choose to equitably share what they have, thus avoiding conflict? We know that this kind of sustainability with peaceful co-existence and the equitable meeting of human needs, as well as a respecting of ecosystem limits, has existed on a small scale, at various times in history and various locations on Earth. Why has it become so difficult, so politically "unrealistic," or "socialist," or "utopian," to even envision or propose such a system at the global level? Why has the founding vision of the United Nations, proclaimed at the end of the most destructive war the world has ever known, "to eliminate forever the scourge of war from human affairs," been so elusive to attain, despite the sincere and good efforts and skills of numerous peacemakers? Is there something else, are there deeper, more ancient behavior patterns at work, residues perhaps of our evolutionary species ancestry, that we can't escape?

Ecological and Evolutionary Aspects of Domination

Examining the question of evolutionary roots of war and domination, we can ask – are there perhaps ancient genetic imprints left over from the evolutionary ancestry of *homo sapiens*, that mammal with three brain systems and an opposable thumb? Can domination and exploitation behavior be observed in the animal realm? Evolutionary biologists have observed that dominance hierarchies, where the males in a pack fight and compete for access to females and resources are common among mammalian and primate species, including our closest genetic relatives, the chimpanzees. The residues of that kind of behavior in human societies are ubiquitous – and can be observed in the authoritarian patriarchal structure of gangs, corporations and political parties. The concept of "alpha males" has entered into the common understanding of media discourse. Dominance hierarchies intersecting with sexist, racist, class, religious and nationalist attitudes of superiority are the focus of ongoing culture struggles and political reform movements throughout the world.

In a recent essay on "A Natural History of Peace," published in *Foreign Affairs,* the well-known evolutionary biologist Robert Sapolsky, reviewing several decades of research in primatology, wrote that the earlier view of humans being inherently and irredeemably violent "killer apes," has had to be revised (Sapolsky, 2006). Our evolutionary heritage is more complex and differentiated. There are indeed primate species, including the chimps, with whom we share 98% of our DNA, who manifest an extraordinary amount of aggression and violence, both within their troop and toward other troops of chimps. On the other hand, there is another branch of the chimpanzee family, the West

African bonobos, who have a uniquely peaceful social system in which conflicts are resolved by cooperative sexual pleasuring, instead of aggressive fighting – surely a hopeful sign (De Waal and Lanting, 1997).

According to Sapolsky, there is striking variation in social practices across primate species: "some primate species, it turns out, are indeed simply violent or peaceful, with that behavior driven by their social structures and ecological settings. More important, however, some primate species can make peace despite violent traits that seem built into their natures. The challenge now is to figure out under what conditions that can happen, and whether humans can manage the trick themselves."[4]

As has often been pointed out, for 99% of human history, humans have lived in small, stable bands of related hunter-gatherers, an ideal setting for the emergence of cooperative behavior, especially in environments in which food sources are abundant. But even in large nation states, history can override deep-seated territorial rivalries. One need only consider the Scandinavian nations, whose military adventurism in the Viking Age and beyond was legendary, but who have become models of caring, socialist peacefulness. The aggressive war-making among monarchies and nation-states which dominated European history for several centuries, has become inconceivable as the new confederation model makes boundary crossings quaint relics of a bygone age.

In attempting to understand the evolutionary roots of domination and violence, some have speculated about the possible residues in human genetic memory of the millions of years of competitive interaction between predators and prey. The ecologist Paul Shepard has argued that predator carnivores have evolved a different kind of consciousness, a different quality of attention, from the prey herbivores, related to their different lives of chasing or escaping (Shepard, 1978). Predator intelligence is searching, aggressive, tuned to stalking and hunting. Prey intelligence is cautious, expectant, ready for instant flight. Omnivore primates and hominids, our own direct ancestors, inherited both kinds of adaptation, both kinds of basic attitude. Is it possible that these different styles of awareness, these opposing modes of relating, form a kind of evolutionary template for the human behavior of aggressors (predators) and victims (prey)? Don't we still hunt, prey on and victimize our fellow humans for survival? Don't we still, in the paranoid mode, instinctive for those preyed upon, vigilantly watch for threats, prepared to flee or defend? At the collective, social level, mega-corporations stalk and hunt for "opening of new markets," or for smaller corporations that may be "ripe for take-over."

In natural ecosystems, the relations between predators and prey species seem to maintain a kind of overall balance in the long run, although that balance is subject to disruption by climate and environment changes. Predation is a primary evolutionary adaptation of certain species, including the human. In the pre-historic transition known as the agricultural revolution, the hunting of other (mostly smaller) animals gave way to herding, and the gathering of plants to growing and gardening. The domestication and slaughtering of animals for food can basically be understood as institutionalized predation. However, we also have the deep genetic memory of having been food for other large mammals. Some believe that the memory of having been a hunted prey stimulated in humans the determination to use their reasoning and technological capabilities to vault themselves to the top of the food chain – where all other animal beings, as well as plants, are seen as potential food sources, to be consumed and exploited.

We need to observe that the killing of the being of another animal species for food is a completely different kind of interaction, than intra-species killing for other motives. We do not judge the violence visited by the lion on the gazelle as evil, nor do we judge the animal killing of the slaughter-house as evil (although we may rightly decry certain methods of killing as "inhumane"). But when a criminal preys on a weaker female or child, raping and murdering, or kills another human being, our moral instincts as well as the ethical principles of all religions are violated. Civilization means having a system of enforceable laws to control such transgressions at the individual and small group level.

No such controls exist, however, to curb predation by rogue kingdoms, nations and empires – although many attempts have been made, through the ages, to establish supra-ordinate legal institutions by agreement, most recently the much-maligned United Nations. The historical record show that again and again, when war or "civil war" breaks out, the moral and legal codes that restrain greed and violence collapse, and the civilized order collapses into barbarism, where there is unrestricted violent predatory competition for resources and mass-murder of civilians.

Besides herding animals for food, humans have also herded medium-sized animals, including other humans, for the work-energy involved, as "energy-slaves," to use an expression coined by Buckminster Fuller. The origin of slavery is historically closely related and analogous to the domestication of animals: both involve the idea of treating another being as property – to be used for doing work. Wherever did humans get such an idea? Unlike killing an animal for food, this is not a phenomenon that prehistoric hominids could have observed in the animal kingdom. There are competitive and cooperative relationships, within and between species. But the practice of enslaving and using other beings for their mechanical or material value only, with no respect for their spiritual essence and autonomy, seems to be unique to humans (with the possible exception of some ants and other insects).

Of course, not all use of domestic animals as beasts of burden is necessarily exploitative and disrespectful – small scale traditional farming and herding comes to mind. And also, not all cultures practiced animal domestication as an adaptation: the indigenous peoples of the Americas chose to domesticate numerous species and varieties of edible plants, but very few animals – maybe the dog and the llama. The Plains Indians, while living in complete symbiotic interdependence with the giant herds of wild buffalo, never domesticated and corralled them.

Capitalism as Organized Predation

In many ways, one could say that capitalism, as it has developed in the past 400 years, and particularly in its industrial corporate form, in the 19th and 20th centuries in the West, is an institutionalized system of slavery and predation: one sub-group of the human species, which itself is only one part of the immensely diverse Earth community of human and other life-forms, elects to survive and adapt by means of accumulation and domination – in other words, taking what they want, for themselves, using force. This self-selected elite group (or gang, or class) – let's call them the techno-industrial corporate humans – consider themselves superior to all other beings on Earth, including the vast majority of other humans, who are thought of as "lower classes," "inferior races," or simply – "the masses."

The elites point to their technological accomplishments, which are indeed stupendous, as well as their economic success, as obvious signs of their general superiority. Other animals and some other classes of human beings are treated as energy-slaves, to be used and exploited for their material bodies, or their work — the "wage-slavery of the helplessly well-employed," in Wendell Berry's eloquent phrase. In addition to some animals and some humans, plants, minerals and metals, and entire ecosystems, are regarded as "resources" to be exploited. Certain mineral and metal materials are built into machines, which can then substitute for human or animal labor, making the actual beings disposable, thus reducing labor costs for the corporation and increasing profits even more.

The officially-promulgated theory of capitalist enterprise does not, of course, see the system from this perspective. According to the theory, there are producers – corporations with limited liability – and consumers, who buy the commodities that the producers consume. According to the theory, it looks like an exchange – everyone gets what they want. Changing prices in a "free market" are supposed to reflect the changing relationships of supply and demand. However, when we look at the way money actually flows in the system, and notice how capitalism enormously increases the inequality of wealth distribution in society, a different picture emerges. We can see how, in actuality, the consumers (people) are consumed by the corporate producers. Observe the people streaming into a WalMart or other megamall: they are being efficiently robbed, having large sums of money extracted from their wallets or bank accounts, all the while being soothed and titillated by the audio-visual blandishments of the advertising industry. The signs that say SAVE or SAVINGS, are actually intended to persuade you to BUY – which is the opposite of saving. They are the economic equivalent of the sign above the entrance to the Auschwitz death-camp: "Work makes Free."

The social-cultural domination system we know as techno-industrial capitalism, involves structured mechanical transformations, using slave or machine labor, of Nature's biological, material and energetic resources into profitable commodities and waste, or cash and trash. Capitalism's psychological root motivation appears to be a kind of addictive fixation on the monetary value of products, called *commodity fetishism*, in Marx's insightful phrase. At the level of economics. this dynamic translates as capital accumulation, driven to grow with relentless and ruthless momentum and ever-increasing concentration, from the local to the national to the global scale. At the level of politics, the capitalist project is dependent on domination by force, and thus increasingly pushes societies into authoritarian and dictatorial forms of social organization, i.e. fascism and imperialism.

From the point of view of the ecological web of life, it should be noted that this industrial project is a linear and irreversible transformation, completely unlike any of the cyclical transformations that we observe in the non-human natural world, where nothing is ever wasted or thrown away and everything is re-used and recycled. Nature's organic processes flow in self-organizing, self-maintaining, regenerative, inter-connected, multidimensional cycles of sacred beauty and infinitely mysterious complexity.

Defenders of the so-called "free-market" system of capitalist enterprise often like to think and say that not only has this system been successful, there are simply no viable alternatives. There are, however, other forms of social organization that have existed in the historical past and still exist, albeit on a small, community scale in various locales to this day. The two main alternative social orders to the capitalist system are the indigenous and the socialist. Some indigenous societies did have priestly and monarchical power hierarchies, while others evolved cooperative, non-dominator models of resource sharing and ecosystem preservation. And socialism, while it may never have existed in a fully realized form at the state level, has been practiced in small-scale cooperative communities, and at least presents the ideal of a social order in which the meeting of all human needs in the society is made the primary goal and value.

Societies attempting to live by such human and environmental value systems are unlikely to find the capitalist systematic domination and exploitation agenda appealing, no matter how dressed up in the philosophical and religious ideology of the ruling elites. Obviously, slaves tend to not like slavery, though they may indeed come to accept it in order to survive, and even to internalize it psychologically. Both a dominator complex and a victim complex may come to reside within the same individual, as psychiatrists know well. To overcome internal resistance by the working classes, the ruling classes in modern nation states, convinced of the rightness and superiority of their way of life, have found it expedient to adopt the violent methods of their ancestor rulers to impose their domination and control agendas, internally against their own people as well as externally against others.

Violent suppression of internal dissent and resistance, coupled with imposed militaristic uniformity of expression and behavior is the political system we call 'fascism' in modern times. Benito Mussolini, credited with its invention, actually said that fascism should better be called "corporatism," pointing to the alliance between the military and the corporations in a fascist system. It is easy to see how the authoritarian command systems required in the military also suit capitalist corporations' push toward uniformity of consumer behavior.

Whereas fascism is the systemic political expression of domination within the nation state, its external expression in international relations is imperialism/colonialism. Invasion, expropriation (plunder), colonization and war have been the dominators' *modus operandi* from the warrior-chieftains of ancient times, to the absolutist monarchies of medieval times and the globe-spanning corporate empires of the modern age. Wars of aggression, invasion and plunder amount to criminal behaviors ("armed robbery," "assault and battery," "breaking and entering") at the level of international relations. Behaviors that are penalized as crimes at the level of a community, are considered appropriate political strategies, *realpolitik*, at the level of relations between nations. This obvious illogical inconsistency has profoundly unjust and destructive consequences for all of humanity.

Capitalism and Imperialism

As was pointed out by Marx and Engels over a hundred years ago, imperialism is the natural outgrowth of monopoly capitalism, with its relentless push toward ever expanding markets. The fact that aggressive imperialist agendas are often supported by resort to self-serving, quasi-religious ideologies, that bring irrational qualities of fanaticism and zealotry to such activities, as well as a kind of sacrificial cult of heroism and martyrdom, does not change the basic fact that the occurrence of war represents the failure of civilization.

It is easy to understand how a society that is invaded and colonized by superior force of arms cannot preserve its existing social order. The peaceful Goddess-centered societies of Old Europe were no match for the armed, horse-mounted Kurgan warriors from Central Asia; just as the peaceful native peoples of the Caribbean were no match for the Spanish conquistadors with their swords and dogs and guns; and the indigenous Dravidians of India no match for the Aryans invading from the North. Historical and present-day examples of imperialist wars of aggression and violent colonization, accompanied by massive killing, plunder, ethnic cleansing and environmental degradation, can be multiplied *ad nauseam*.

When I was writing my book *The Well of Remembrance* (Metzner, 1994), I discovered that some of the oldest myths of the original Indo-Europeans, who were nomadic herders, are the myths of divinely inspired cattle raiding – myths that lived on in the American Old West, with its ubiquitous stories of ranchers and rustlers. Some historians trace the early beginnings of capital accumulation to the enclosures movement in 16th century England, when powerful landowners, supported by soldiers, put a fence around grazing land that had previously been considered the wealth of the commons, and started charging rent for its use (Snyder, 1990). Different groups of gangster capitalists ("robber barons") compete and fight with one another: Spanish ships that sailed to the New World, taking gold from the natives, were assaulted on the high seas by English pirates, who found it convenient to add to their hoard by stealing that of another pirate ship.

In our time, mega-corporations and their state backers aggressively expand their power and wealth by mergers and "take-overs" of the production systems of other corporations. In the post-Cold War period of the dominance of the US as the "sole superpower" we have seen the relentless globalization of the capitalist neo-liberal model, even to the extent of taking over the public infrastructure of entire countries, basically stealing their natural resources and devastating the local economy and ecology.

Imperialism and colonialism involves one dominant state or nation taking the resource base of another, and imposing their rule on the subject population, exacting tribute or taxes. Genocide, from the perspective of the dominators, is simply a strategy for removing an entire population from a certain area, and replacing it with another population, which then takes over the existing resources. The cost of maintaining the original population is reduced or eliminated by extermination.

In our time, we have economic imperialism, dressed up in the camouflage terminology of "free trade" and "development," which takes the form of privatization – where large multi-national corporations take over the common wealth of a society or country (water, utilities, infrastructure, etc). Increasingly, the enormous wealth accumulated by the huge corporations (especially those involved in oil, ore, minerals and other primary resources, as well as military contractors), enables them to pursue their own growth agenda, using shadowy, behind-the-scenes, extra-legal maneuvering to free them from democratic controls and accountability. Ensuring the malleability and compliance of national governments becomes, for such multinational gangs, just another "cost of doing business."

In recent times, the Canadian social critic and journalist Naomi Klein has brilliantly exposed the rise of what she calls "disaster capitalism," in which the mega-corporations of the military-industrial complex first profit from the production and sale of arms to the US imperial power. Then, with the help of their governmental clients, promote wars of aggressive invasion that destroy a designated "enemy" country, complete with sophisticated PR campaigns to induce psychological shock and economic paralysis. Finally, these same imperial corporations appropriate the natural resources (oil, forests, minerals, water) of the destroyed nation state into their corporate machines; and then profit further from being given "no-bid" contracts to rebuild the shattered infra-structure of the defeated country (Klein, 2007).

***

We can see how the building of nations and empires is irrevocably connected not only with genocide against various external "others," but also with violence against internal groups, as class warfare and exploitative domination of subject populations. The nagging question remains, how does it happen that societies, from ancient to modern times, have time and again failed to maintain a cooperative social order and have fallen victim to being taken over by tyrannical, war-like and imperialist elites, often with the complicity of priests, intellectuals and ideologues?

We have examined the roots of domination behavior in the modern world in deep-seated psychological complexes stemming from child-rearing practices, in ancient historical patterns of tribal competition and in evolutionary residues of mammalian predation. We turn now to consider the possibility that there are hidden forces, secret societies, active in human civilization that push societies repeatedly into divisive and destructive conflicts, deliberately practicing the strategy of "divide and conquer." Even more disturbing is the possibility that there may be supra-human "dark forces," "evil spirits," demonic deities or destructive archetypes, that manipulate human consciousness and historical events for their own domination agendas. It turns out that there is quite a vast body of historical, occult and religious mythological literature that deals with just this question.

A Teaching on "Dark Forces"

I will begin by relating the following extremely vivid dream, that I had a few years ago. While in the dream state I felt no fear, but thinking about it in retrospect, I found the implications terrifying. At the same time, I also felt it offered some insights into the questions of domination, war, violence and evil that I had been thinking about.

I find myself in a gathering of human-like beings that I understand to be a dark force council. There are no discernible facial or other bodily features: I am seeing only the upper torso and heads of about a dozen hooded figures, arranged as if around a table. No lower bodies or legs are visible, nor any differentiating individual features, such as male or female. The faces and torsos of these beings are uniformly shrouded in dark grey veils. For a moment I am questioning myself as to the reason for my presence in this group. Why was I invited, if I was invited? The beings did not seem to notice me or address any communications to me personally. They just emanated a very coherent set of thought-forms, whose meanings I seemed to be able to register telepathically.

The primary thought-form that I picked up was that the sole and exclusive focus of the beings in this council was to accumulate more power and more wealth. More wealth to get more power, more power to get more wealth. To this end they dedicated all of their will power and all their concentration. They prided themselves on their power of concentration, which did indeed seem formidable. There were no distractions and disruptions in the coherency of their mental energy-field.

On awakening, I remembered reading an interview with the CEO of Enron, prior to that corporation's crash into bankruptcy, and their officers' indictment on fraud charges. In the interview, the CEO said that they prided themselves on their "laser-like focus" on increasing earnings-per-share – and nothing else. I have come to think of the beings I saw in my dream vision as "dominator spirits." I'm inclined to think that they "exist" at the mental level of reality, not at the ordinary, material time-space level. But they apparently can inspire and guide the ruling elites, whether monarchical and feudal, or military and corporate, with their single-minded focus on accumulating power and wealth.

I am not saying that the will to gain power or wealth is inherently evil or bad. It is important to recognize, however, that the intention to accumulate wealth and power in the ruling elites is only for their group or class, not the wealth and well-being of the whole society, or the general population. The game of global capitalism is a game of money and power. There are multiple, overlapping conspiracies and agendas – all revolving around a fateful web of forces that define the elites' agendas. Some refer to this as the G-O-D triangle, where G = guns and armaments, O = oil and other carbon fuels, and D = drugs and narcotics. Money flows and accumulates around all three points of this triangle, superseding national interests and laws (Scott, 2003).

For the wealthy ruling class, the scientific quest for knowledge, or service to human needs, or preservation of the environment, are of no concern or interest; or at best, they are secondary to the goal of accumulating power and wealth. People dying is of no concern to the globalizing war corporations and their client states: it's "cost of doing business" for the corporations, "collateral damage" to the military. For other groups and individuals the goals of money and power are secondary, and science, human welfare, environmental preservation are primary goals and values. I am not making absolutist claims here that all corporate leaders are criminal gangsters, or all political leaders would-be tyrants. I know that there are many honest, sincere, intelligent people, working for peace, well-being and justice, at all levels of society. I am trying to understand the complex web of forces that shape human civilization in so many ways, some of them hidden and not well understood. I'm thinking about what it means for the survival and prospering of our civilization, if such hidden power dynamics do in fact exist.

Reflecting on the dream vision, I was at first dismayed at the thought that in order to counter the onslaught of these dominator groups' destructive predatory assault on the rest of humanity and the entire biosphere one would have to match their truly formidable power of concentration, and what a challenge that would be. On further reflection, however, it became clear that the dominators have a much easier concentrative task, since they only have one goal to focus on. They literally don't care about any other values, such as respect for human rights and dignity, justice, equality, preserving the quality of the environment, and so forth. Those human beings and groups that wish to support the unfolding of life, human and non-human, in all its diversity, and the building of sustainable, cooperative societies, have a much greater variety and multiplicity of purposes, and therefore a much more difficult task of concentration. Therefore there is an unjustified element of arrogance in the dominators' claim to superior powers of concentration.

I also realized that the arrogant one-pointed concentration of the dominator spirits and their human vassals, may lead to their undoing. Because of their single-minded focus of attention, they may not perceive internal failings or external threats to their system of power, before it collapses. "Pride comes before destruction," according to the ancient Biblical proverb. Certainly the testimony of history is clear: no empire or tyranny in world history has failed to eventually collapse, either from internal weaknesses, or by external attack, or by exhausting their ecological habitat.

Perhaps these dominator spirits are also the guiding spirits behind various legendary occult secret societies and brotherhoods, such as the *Illuminati*, who are said to manipulate world events behind the scenes, through their direct influence on mass-mind images. In his book *Secret Brotherhoods*, the esoteric philosopher Rudolf Steiner has written about the malevolent influence of hidden forces in human history, particularly the modern era (Steiner, 1917/2004). William Bramley, in his book *The Gods of Eden*, has accumulated an impressive amount of documentary evidence for the existence and activities of such secret groups in world history (Bramley, 1989).

In some esoteric formulations, the forces or spirits that I'm calling dominator spirits, are called "dark force" or "counter-evolutionary." What does it mean to be working with a counter-evolutionary agenda? Evolution, as we know, involves populations of organisms finding habitats or niches to exploit, in which they can unfold their potentials and use creative strategies to meet their survival needs. The dominator spirits and the human beings and groups guided by them, are takers, predators and plunderers, who use violence and warfare to get what they want. Going far beyond meeting their own survival needs, they augment their wealth basically by stealing from others and killing those who resist or obstruct them. Their goal is not the welfare of the whole community or society, but rather to accumulate wealth and power for their own elite family, clan or group.

Dominators, and the institutions created by them, want to grow by accumulating and concentrating wealth quantitatively, rather than growing by fostering the creative and qualitative unfolding of diverse populations and their varying adaptations.

In that sense, it could be said that capital accumulation, fascism, militarism and war are "counter-evolutionary" forces. Those who want to continue supporting diversity and evolutionary unfolding resist such authoritarian domination agendas, and may be moved to take up arms to fight against them. But violent resistance and armed struggle are doomed to ultimate failure, since violence only breeds further violence, and in the end everyone loses, civilization is destroyed and whole countries are made uninhabitable. The dominator spirits and the systems set up by their human intermediaries thrive on war and profit from it, to the point where one could aptly think of it as an addictive pattern, as we have seen.

While I was working on the present essay, some time after the dominator dream related above, I came across a book called *Report from Iron Mountain*, that provided an eerie and unexpected confirmation of these perspectives. Written by an anonymous author (though with an introduction by the critic Leonard Lewin), and published by Dial Press in New York in 1967, the book purports to be the report of a think tank of government, academic and business leaders (none of whom are named) – convened to study the "possibility and desirability of peace," i.e. what would be the consequences of general disarmament scenarios then being considered. It is not known who commissioned the report (though to my mind it has McNamara's signature all over it), who the participants were, or what was done with it. The conclusions of the report were considered so shocking that it was never officially released or publicly discussed – only appearing in this one, anonymous, unsanctioned edition:

> War is not, as is widely assumed, primarily an instrument of policy utilized by nations to extend or defend their expressed political values or their economic interests. On the contrary, it is itself the principal

basis of organization on which all modern societies are constructed. The common proximate cause of war is the apparent interference of one nation with the aspirations of another. But at the root of all ostensible differences of national interest lie the dynamic requirements of the war system itself for armed conflict. Readiness for war characterizes contemporary social systems more broadly than their economic and political structures (Anonymous, 1967).

The report goes on to discuss the non-military functions of the war system, for which any proposed disarmament proposal must provide viable substitutes.[5]

What the report suggests to me is that, in addition to the functions of war to defend a country against external enemies, the war system has by now been integrated so systematically and deeply into all aspects of the modern political economy, based on industrial capitalism, that it is extremely difficult to see one's way out of this consuming predicament. The *Report from Iron Mountain* is, so to speak, the dominators' systems blueprint for society: a fascistic, authoritarian order of total control, focused on stability and conformity, in which all ecological, human, aesthetic, moral and spiritual values and needs are subsidiary.

It is striking too, to what extent this domination blueprint coincides with the *Project for a New American Century*,[6] that has been the underlying ideological program of the neo-conservative group that has taken increasing control of the US government over the last 10 years. Furthermore, it seems clear to me that the domination agenda of both the systems thinkers of the *Report from Iron Mountain* and the neocon imperialistic agenda of the *Project for a New American Century* coincide more or less exactly with what I saw was the underlying mind-set expressed by the "dark force" or counter-evolutionary league in my dream vision.

In my research on the roots of war, I seemed to have arrived at what in many ways are rather pessimistic and depressing observations and conclusions. I did however, find that they liberated me from the last vestiges of an illusory assumption I had held – that everyone obviously wants peace rather than war. I wonder for how many peace movement activists, this kind of assumption functions as a kind of conceptual and perceptual block. The conclusions about the inevitability and desirability of war emerged out of the focused and well-meaning efforts of responsible, intelligent systems thinkers in the most technologically advanced society on Earth today, and the policy statements advocating total global dominance are formulations by the ruling elites presently in control of an immensely powerful military machine. Given these facts, I believe it is essential that those individuals and groups who want peace and work for peace, be clearly aware that there are extremely powerful and influential forces that have the opposite agenda – namely the maintenance and expansion of a permanent global war-system.

* * *

I felt I wanted to investigate further the evidence and esoteric teachings regarding supra-human or archetypal and mythic dimensions of this difficult situation. Perhaps such teachings could shed some light on the apparently insoluble predicament of domination and war.

Mythic Dimensions of Domination and War

I wish now to examine some of these more esoteric as well as mythic perspectives on the roots of war and domination. Other writers interested in the problems of war in society have investigated its mythic dimensions. A notable recent example is the Jungian psychotherapist and scholar James Hillman, now in his 80s, who recently published *A Terrible Love of War* (Hillman, 2005). Hillman says that war is normal, not just usual. It is inhuman in the same way the gods, including Mars and Venus, are inhuman. Venusian qualities of beauty and love belong to war as do the Martian qualities of violence and aggression. Hillman concludes that war is inherent in the existence of states (as do the authors of the *Report from Iron Mountain*) and identifies the exclusive worldviews of the monotheistic religions as a major contributing factor.

In my own research, I have been led to a view that recognizes at least two (or possibly more) kinds of archetypal forces or spirits guiding and inspiring the lives of individuals and societies. One group are those who support the peaceful, creative unfolding of life's evolutionary potentials and the preservation of the planet's life-support system. The pursuit of knowledge and the development of technology is integrated with respect for all living beings, and reverence for the spiritual reality of the universe. The other kind are those who have chosen the adaptation of accumulating and taking from others, using violence and war, and can thus be aptly described as counter-evolutionary. I would like now to examine some mythic and legendary prototypes of this kind of dualistic heritage.

World mythology is filled with stories of rival brother gods, such as the Egyptian Osiris and Seth, the Sumerian Enlil and Enki, or the Zoroastrian Ahura-Mazda and Ahriman. Some myths tell of feuding groups of deities, such as the *Aesir* and *Vanir* of the Norse people, and of battles between "gods" and "titans" or "monsters," found on planet Earth in earlier times. In both Hindu and Buddhist mythology, we have the conception of *devas* and *asuras* – the former beneficent light-beings, the latter violent and destructive dominators. Both are supra-human spirits, inhabiting their own worlds, which nevertheless intersect and interact with the world of humans in multiple and complex ways.

The persistent legend of the high civilization of Atlantis, which is said to have collapsed in a catastrophic flood, about ten or twelve thousand years before our time, also has this theme of a struggle between highly advanced beings, some creative and constructive and another group on an imperialistic and exploitative path. In our time, such myths have been given new formulations in the literature on UFOs and ETs, where the rival "gods" of ancient times are technologically highly advanced beings from extra-terrestrial civilizations who have been intervening in human affairs for a very long time.

Buddhist Myths of Devas and Asuras

Buddhism is basically a non-theistic religion, in which the essential moral teachings involve not so much an appeal to a book of rules handed down by an omnipotent creator and his priesthood, but rather the exhortation to practice meditative yogic methods designed to raise consciousness. Moral and peaceful behavior would then follow naturally from the inner peace and equanimity of a person who is in touch with their true essential nature, their "Buddha nature." Unconsciousness or ignorance of one's own spiritual essence, along with craving and hatred, are the "three poisons" at the core of all human life. They are symbolized by the three inter-linked animals (snake, rooster and pig) at the hub of the great ever-cycling Wheel of Birth and Death.

Buddhism did adopt and adapt some of the key cosmological myths of their Vedic and Hindu religious ancestors, including the conceptions of *devas* and *asuras*. Devas are the "shining ones," light spirits, analogous to "angels" in Western religion. They guide and inspire humans in their artistic and creative endeavors, and remind them of their spiritual essence. Asuras are violent and envious demons, armed with weapons, focused on materiality, who are forever competing with the devas and attacking all forms of life in general. Whereas in the Indian Vedic (and related Persian Zoroastrian) mythology the focus is on the competition and struggle between the light and dark, good and evil, deities, Buddhism developed a more sophisticated analysis expressed in the symbolism of the six worlds of existence (*samsara*), linked by the twelve-fold chain of interdependent causation.

The iconic image of the *Wheel of Samsara*, which could also be called the Wheel of Earthly Existence, as portrayed in numerous temple paintings throughout the Buddhist world, is held in the grip of a gigantic black demon, representing the ceaseless flow of time and entropy. At the hub of the churning wheel are the three "poisons" (unconsciousness, craving and hatred) and around the outside rim of the wheel are the twelve links of the chain of interdependent mutual causation. The six worlds of possible existence are arrayed around the wheel, turning ceaselessly in cycles of birth, death and rebirth. These worlds can be regarded as realms of consciousness and reality inhabited by various beings, both human and non-human.

One of the six realms is specifically designated the human realm, and is considered the most favorable realm for humans –because it has the greatest freedom of choice and therefore possibilities for liberation. Human beings may be incarnated into any of the six realms, in any given life-time, according to their karma; and within one life-time, humans can find themselves, temporarily, in the state of consciousness associated with that realm (Metzner, 1996). Our spiritual growth challenge then is to recognize and identify the world we are inhabiting by raising consciousness. Thus we learn to gradually free ourselves from the thrall of the three poisons.

One of the six worlds is the world of animals: this does not mean that humans may reincarnate as animals, as some simplistic beliefs hold. It means rather that we, as human beings, are essentially living in the consciousness of the animal realm, along with the animal spirits, when we are focused exclusively on instinctual mammalian survival programs. There is also a realm of *pretas* – "hungry ghosts," with huge bellies and thin throats, forever craving and forever frustrated. This could be considered an apt symbolic portrayal of the realm of humans fixated in addictive and obsessive states of consciousness.

The realm inhabited by the devas is an angelic world of great natural and aesthetic beauty, peace and harmony. Heaven, in the Buddhist conception, is not so much a realm we may enter into after we die. It is, like all states, a temporary state into which we come by good karma and spiritual disciplines. We are in the deva realm when we are in heavenly, blissful states of consciousness.

There is a hell world, opposite on the Wheel of Samsara, which is marked by extreme pain, suffering and victimization. "Hell" may be a purely subjective state of painful illness or madness; or it may also be experienced in an objective environment of war, torture and violence. In Buddhism, heaven is not a promised after-life reward and hell is not a threatened punishment – both are impermanent states of consciousness. We are *in* these realms for varying lengths of time, or perhaps sometimes for an entire lifetime, in accordance with the law of choices and consequences (*karma*).

In the image of the Wheel of Existance, the deva deities are sitting peacefully in a garden setting, an ecological paradise, full of flowering plants, peaceful lakes and musicians playing. The asura realm is located next to the deva realm on the Wheel, and the asuras are shown as horse-mounted, armed warriors, brandishing their weapons and howling with frightful noise. In an image eerily symbolic of our present ecological catastrophe, where industrial mega-corporations backed by military gangs are devouring the rainforests and other biosphere resources, the asuras are cutting down the fruit-laden giant tree that the deva gods are contemplating and enjoying.

Opposite the asura realm on the Wheel of Samsara, lies the realm of the addicted and frustrated pretas. This could also be regarded as a symbolic portrayal of the global situation, where massively armed and violent gangs amass huge illicit profits from trafficking in drugs which hold millions in addictive bondage. The asuras correspond most closely to what I (and other writers) have called dominator or counter-evolutionary, or "dark force" spirits.

In both the Hindu and Buddhist cosmology, the devas,

the spirits of peace and sustainability, and asuras, the spirits of violence and domination, are present in human civilization and history in varying proportions. According to Indian traditions, there are cosmic cyclical ages, the *yugas*, extending over tens of thousands of years, in which either the peaceful devas or the violent asuras are more prominent. Modern researchers like John Major Jenkins, in his work *Galactic Alignment* (Jenkins, 2002), relate these ages to the 26,000 year cycle of precession. All sources agree that the present age, the Kali Yuga, is the climax or low point, of an age ruled by the war-like asuras. The fact that for most of recorded history, at least in the past 6,000 years, since the Kurgan intrusions into Old Europe, Western societies have been ruled by warrior-chiefs, autocratic monarchs and emperors, and in our time, military juntas, gives this conception an undeniable plausibility.

As far as I know, the Buddhists, while recognizing the transience of all rulers and empires, do not have a cosmic time-table for the change-over from one age to another. They would say that, both for the individual and for societies, the balance of peaceful and violent forces is a matter of the choices made by human individuals, and the groups to which they belong. Undoubtedly, the certain knowledge of the transience of all phenomena, including political ones, would help one to maintain equanimity and dignity even in the face of the most outrageous violations of human decency and morality, and to continue to counter the virulent depredations of the asuras and their human incarnations. Whether the defense against armed predatory plunder will inevitably lead to continuing cycles of violence and vengeance, or whether war can be countered and contained by active, yet non-violent struggle for peace and sustainability, may be the central challenge of our planetary civilization.

The Legend of the Downfall of the Civilization of Atlantis

A vast literature exists, ranging from the scientific and scholarly, to the speculative and mediumistic, telling of a lost civilization on an island in the Atlantic, that was so completely destroyed, with all its records, in a cataclysmic flood, that it has been lost to historical memory. As a proto-historical legend, the story of Atlantis was first recorded in the 5th century BCE by the Athenian Plato, the god-father of Western philosophy, who said he heard the story from ancient Egyptian sources. In the 20th century, the Atlantis legend was revived in a major way by the gifted American psychic Edgar Cayce, who left a multitude of paranormally channeled readings concerning Atlantis (Hope, 1991).

According to Cayce and other psychic pre-historians, Atlantis was a civilization with a naval empire, whose ships dominated the globe, engaging (in its later stages) in plundering warfare with various other societies, including the Athenian, as recorded by Plato. The empire was ruled by a theocratic priesthood of humans with highly advanced psychic abilities, vastly extended life-spans and extraordinarily advanced technology of genetic engineering. Later myths told of these beings as "gods," because of their apparent "immortality" (actually supra-human longevity), and seemingly supernatural capacities. Esoteric mystical schools of modern times call them high-level initiates, adept at working with the energies of multiple dimensions of consciousness and reality. Atlantean scientists apparently mastered technologies based on crystals and sound vibrations, both for building pyramids and military weaponry.

Some of these high-level adepts had chosen a "dark force" path of sorcery and exploitation, using their super-human abilities to create animal-human hybrids for the purposes of work or sexual slavery. Others in the ruling priesthood adhered to a mystical path of oneness and respect for all beings, and attempted to counteract or ameliorate the depredations of the dark force dominators. In the modern channelled ET literature, it is often proposed that the Atlanteans actually came to Earth from another star-system (Sirius being a favored candidate), for the purpose of establishing colonies on Earth.

In accounting for the downfall of this powerful global empire, there are several versions: one is a classic "punishment of the wicked" scenario, as in the Biblical legend of the Great Flood, in which the karmic consequences of the dark ones' activities came back to destroy them. Other writers point to the physical and geographical evidence that there actually were planet-wide catastrophes around the 11th and 10th millennium BCE – and suggest that the Atlantean technocrats were blind to the consequences of their physical interventions on the Earth's energy-systems. In either case, so the story goes, those of the ruling elites who could see the catastrophe coming, years ahead of time, sent out expeditions to establish settlements in different parts of the world. Here the indigenous people were taught the rudiments of the Atlantean sacred science, and structures were built (for example, pyramids) containing coded records of this high civilization. This activity is then said to have led to the beginnings of the ancient Egyptian, Meso-American, Northwestern European and perhaps other civilizations.

One psychic pre-historian that I came to know, stated that

a number of souls of the Atlantean scientists who had been
involved in the hyper-development of the physical, biological,
and psychical technologies of that empire, were now reincarnated,
again as visionary scientists and engineers, to try to prevent
the same or similar misuses occurring again. Undeniably, there
are eerie parallels between the putative pre-collapse situation
of Atlantis, and our own time, where the dominator forces of
techno-industrial exploitation are pushing the Earth's ecosystems
to the brink of collapse, while scientific and environmental
groups and their allies, struggle to build and maintain sustainable
communities at a local and regional scale.

The Wars of the Gods in Norse Mythology

In the religious mythology of the Nordic-Germanic people,
there is fascinating evidence for the interaction between the
Indo-European Kurgan invaders and the Old European cultures.
We find this in the myths of the prolonged warfare and eventual
peacemaking between two families of deities, the Aesir and
the Vanir. I have discussed these myths in my book *The Well
of Remembrance*, basing my interpretation on the archaeo-
mythological work of Marija Gimbutas (Metzner, 1994). She
has proposed, on the basis of the archaeological record, that the
invasions of the Indo-European nomadic herder tribes called
Kurgans into the agrarian matricentric cultures of Old Europe,
starting in the 5th millennium BCE, led to initial warfare, and
eventual hybridizing of cultures and religious worldviews. In this
kind of approach to the interpretation of mythology, ancient
stories and epics are seen as recordings of even more ancient oral
traditions concerning actual events in pre-historic times, often

overlaid with fantastic elaborations. Such a view of mythology is consistent with that of Robert Graves, Mircea Eliade, and Zachariah Sitchin, whose work on Sumerian myth we shall discuss further below.

According to the Nordic-Germanic mythic history, there were two families or clans of deities, the *Aesir* and the *Vanir*. The Aesir were primarily sky- and warrior-gods, including Odin, Tiwaz and Thor the Thunderer. The Vanir, including Nerthus, Njörd and the brother-sister pair Freyr and Freyja, were primarily earth- and nature-deities, associated with prosperity and peace. The two groups of gods were portrayed in the myths as warring rivals, although there are also stories of peacemaking attempts and cooperation. Presumably these myths reflect the conflict, drawn out over many centuries, between the invading Indo-Germanic tribes from the East and the aboriginal populations of Old Europe, who resisted the attempted assimilation. It seems probable that after the Indo-Germanic people had settled in Central Europe, the Vanir continued to be the gods of the farmers and fishermen, while the Aesir were worshipped by the military aristocracy, who had appropriated the land and established their domination.

In *The Eddas*, the mythic poems that are our prime source for the Nordic myths, the Aesir envied and craved the wealth of the Vanir, and "thus war came into the world." The archaeological evidence from the cultures of Old Europe shows that it was in fact the patriarchal Kurgan or Aryan invaders, with their sky- and battle-gods and gleaming weapons, who brought warfare to the peaceful agrarian societies, with their deities of fertility, abundance and peace. The new religion that the descendants of both peoples developed was a hybrid of Eurasian shamanic warrior cults and the earth-based fertility magic of the indigenous inhabitants.

For the migrating Indo-Germanic people, the lands to the West were fabulously rich and fertile lands, where they could graze their herds and learn farming from the indigenous people. Both peoples had developed the arts of extracting metals such as copper, bronze, gold and iron from the earth, and gold was highly prized for its malleability in shaping shining ornaments. The wealth, both agrarian and mineral, of the peaceful cultures of Old Europe, personified in the figure of *Gullveig*, the "Golden Goddess," undoubtedly did arouse the greed and envy of the rapacious invaders. Gold seems to have been an obsession for the Indo-Europeans wherever they went, including the Spaniards and Portuguese who invaded the Americas – an obsession that has triggered more than one blood-drenched military adventure.

The characterization of the Aesir as attacking and invading the lands of the Vanir out of rapacious envy for their wealth, parallels the mythic imagery of the asuras as "envious titans" attacking the fruit-laden tree of abundant life that the devas are peacefully enjoying. The names *Aesir* and *asuras* may actually have same linguistic root, according to some scholars. The idea that it is the "gods" who bring war into the world, and drag their human followers into their competitive struggle, is one we will encounter again in Zachariah Sitchin's work on Sumerian mythology.

Extra-terrestrial Ruler "Gods" in Sumerian Mythology

The idea that the "gods" of ancient times and myths were actually human-like visitors from highly advanced extra-terrestrial civilizations, who established colonies on Earth, features in the work of several writers, most notably that of Israeli scholar Zachariah Sitchin. The Sumerian city-state civilization appeared, without any evidence of a gradual development, about 3500 years BCE, with agriculture, building, irrigation, mathematics, a highly sophisticated calendar and astronomy. So there is a real unresolved question among pre-historians and Sumerologists, as to the origin of this civilization. The Sumerians themselves, when asked by later historians where they obtained their knowledge, replied "from the *Anunaki*," which means "those who came down from above" – in other words, they were what we would nowadays call extra-terrestrials. A similar word occurs in the Biblical *Book of Genesis*: usually translated as "giants" the Hebrew word *nephilim* actually means "those who came down from above."

Sitchin made an exhaustive many decades-long study of original cuneiform writings (and associated images inscribed in clay tablets) in Sumerian and other Mesopotamian languages, tracing stories of the relations between gods and humans in the various myths. Comparing them with the stories in the Hebrew Bible, Sitchin found the latter were heavily redacted versions of much more extensive earlier originals. Instead of interpreting the ancient myths symbolically, as fables, Sitchin decided to read them as records of actually observed, historic events. He has detailed his findings in six volumes of a series he calls *The Earth Chronicles*. The first of these, *The Twelfth Planet*, was published in the 1970s; *Genesis Revisited*, published twenty years later, compared the readings from Sumerian myth with the latest findings in astronomy and genetics (Sitchin, 1976; 1990). Biological anthropologist Arthur David Horn, in his book *Humanity's Extra-Terrestrial Origins* (Horn, 1994), examines the standard scientific theories of human evolution, with its puzzles and questions, and offers a sober-minded consideration of the alternative suggested by Sitchin and other researchers, that visitors from other worlds (and other dimensions) have played a significant role in the evolution of human life and culture on planet Earth. I will try to summarize the rather huge amount of literature on this topic, particularly as it relates to the question of the origins of war and domination.

According to Sitchin's reading of the Sumerian texts, the Anunaki were a technologically advanced race of large humanoids from the planet Nibiru, a large planet in the far outer reaches of our solar system – which is as yet undetected by astronomers, although some indirect evidence for the existence of such a planet is being reported. Because of the extreme length of Nibiru's solar orbit, the Annunaki lived for thousands of years in Earth time, which accounts for the belief that they were "immortal." They possessed space-ships, some of them armed with weapons, reports of sightings of which can be found in abundance in ancient Middle-Eastern mythology, including the Bible (Schellhorn, 1989). They arrived on Earth about 500,000 years ago, to set up mining colonies, building cities with step-pyramids as landing platforms for their space-ships.

Needing workers for their gold mines, they genetically engineered a hybrid between an upright-walking indigenous bi-pedal primate and Anunaki stock. This is the meaning behind the strange line in *Genesis*, "Let us create an Adamah ("earthling") in our own image and likeness." The line is strange because, in a text devoted to the activities of a solo creator god, there is suddenly a reference to a group. Apparently, fragments from the original stories at times survived the editing of the Hebrew priests.

The creator scientists responsible for this genetic breeding program were the god Enki (or Ea), and his consort Ninharsag. There are pictures inscribed on clay tablets of Enki holding a chemical flask, and his consort holding a baby on her lap. Enki was the first-born son of the supreme god Anu, and the first ruler of the Earth colony. He was a scientist whose relationship to his creations was that of a benevolent teacher. After some years, Enki's brother Enlil, who although younger, was the first son of Anu's official spouse, was sent to Earth to administer the colonies. There was sibling rivalry between the brother gods, and in general considerable competitive family-feuding among the Anunaki. (This is a feature of much ancient mythology that is hard to explain in symbolic terms, but makes eminent sense if the myths are actually histories). Where Enki was a benevolent teacher, Enlil carried out his assignment as a stern, demanding law-giver.

For tens of thousands of years, these rival brother gods and their respective descendants, were the dominant beings on this planet, founding and presiding over the Sumerian, Babylonian, Assyrian, Egyptian, Indian and perhaps even Meo-American civilizations.

Since hybrids don't reproduce, the new earthlings still did not fully meet the labor shortages of the Anunaki. So Enki and Ninharsag proposed at the council of the gods, that they re-engineer the Adam to come in two sexes, and teach them to reproduce themselves. Enlil, who was by this time in charge of the plantation called EDIN, opposed this suggestion, and forbade his charges to partake of the fruit of the knowledge tree, nor the tree of long life (because then they "would be like one of us"). The Anunaki scientists first modified the gene stock to add the distaff side (taking a "rib from Adam's left side"), then secretly taught the man and woman reproductive sex. This was necessary because primates and other mammals reproduce instinctively, not with conscious intention; hence the biblical association of "knowing" with "sex."

The Bible states that sexual knowledge was given to Adam and Eve by the Serpent. The allusion to the serpent might mean (a) that Enki and other Annunaki had some reptilian features; or (b) that the myths called the one who taught sexual knowledge the serpent, because the serpent was Enki's emblem (appropriately, for a genetic engineer); (c) later redactors of the *Book of Genesis* wrote the role of Enki completely out of the Bible, and demonized him as a deceptive snake – a common practice in the writing of histories and myths. From henceforth there would be only one "god," not a family or a council, to be obeyed and served – particularly for the "people chosen" by that one god. The origin of ancient Hebrew monotheism was thus by *fiat* from Yahweh, the current ruler god, who was in the Enlil lineage.

When Enlil found out what had happened, he was furious, cursed the female, the snake and the Earth, and expelled the pair from Eden, telling them that they would have to fend for themselves. No longer would they have the easy life on the garden plantation ("of every tree in the garden you may freely eat, except..."). Thus, the "Fall from Eden" can be read as the first slave rebellion, assisted by a sympathetic insider among the rulers. The now paired humans had declared their autonomy and were forced into taking responsibility for their own survival. As the newly created humans multiplied, their females provided attractive sexual mates for male Anunaki – the offspring of these matings being the demi-gods and long-lived super-heroes of various mythologies. This racial inter-breeding is referred to in the infamous lines in *Genesis*, that evidently also escaped the eyes of the redactors: "the sons of god found the daughters of men fair, and had children by them, giants upon the Earth, and mighty men of old." (*Gen*, 6:3)

From the mythology of the Sumerians as interpreted by Sitchin, we find that feuding between branches of the Anunaki families, together with their mixed Anunaki-human descendants continued for thousands of years. Male humans were drafted into military service for their rulers, who fought pitched battles by land, sea and air. The mythology of Vedic India, as well as the Egyptian and Sumero-Babylonian abounds with long, detailed descriptions of battles between the gods (like Horus and Set), in flying ships with fiery laser-beam weapons and their human foot-soldiers (Sitchin, 1985). Selected human females were drafted into personal housekeeping or sexual services for the ruler gods, or for breeding demi-god heroes – as told in the stories of Zeus and his many human lovers, or Innana/Ishtar and her chosen royal lover.

By time the Anunaki left, perhaps when the legendary flood wiped out the great cities they had established, humans had learned to colonize, dominate and enslave other populations – from the overlords who had genetically engineered and enslaved their remote ancestors in the first place. Here is a key to the understanding of the roots of domination: *humans may have learned to dominate other humans from the extra-terrestrial overlords who dominated them.* The master-slave dichotomy was built in, perhaps genetically, but certainly by socialization, from the very beginnings of the human species. In a similar way, we have seen in the 20th century, that the ruling elites in countries formerly colonized by European nations, proceeded to enslave and exploit the poorer working classes in their newly independent nations. And at the level of the family, as we know, children who are abused and mistreated by adults, are likely to learn to abuse and mistreat their children and those less powerful, when they grow up.

There are formidable obstacles in the minds of most people to accepting even the possibility that this story might contain some important truths. For me personally, I found these perspectives initially unbelievable and unsettling, but ultimately liberating and exciting because they helped me to understand some of the really strange behaviors of civilized Earth humans, including the persistence of war and domination and the connection with religious belief systems.

If we really are the descendants of genetic hybrid earthlings bred as slaves, and the dichotomies of *master/slave, predator/ prey* and *perpetrator/victim* were built into the human genome as unconscious predispositions, then the evolutionary and spiritual challenge is to free our minds from the thralldom of this religious conditioning. "Breaking the god spell" is how Neil Freer, a long-term student of Sitchin's work framed the task for awakening humanity (Freer, 1987). It is important too to remember that the pre-flood history of gods and humans includes not only the legacy of Enlil, the demanding law-giver, but also that of Enki, the beneficent scientist and teacher.

The lineage that stems from Enlil includes the Egyptian

deities Ra and Set, the Hebrew Yahweh, the Vedic Indra and Vishnu, the Greek Zeus, the Norse Aesir like Odin and Thor, the Islamic Allah, the Christian Father-God and others. They are patriarchal law-giver gods, who rule by command, sometimes with a "holy book" of rules, and emphasize fear and the threat of punishment. They appear to have a war-like, violent and controlling disposition, especially Yahweh, and the Buddhist Asuras.

The Enki lineage of creator gods, scientists and teachers, include the Egyptian gods Ptah, Thoth, Osiris, the Hebrew Elohim, the Greek Hermes and Dionysus, the Indian Shiva, the Norse Vanir like Freyja and Freyr (though Odin belongs in this camp also, as knowledge-seeking god of shamans), the Feathered Serpent Quetzalcoatl in Mexico and others. They are benevolent and beneficent towards humans, supportive of diversity and creativity, and inclusive of the feminine goddesses – as portrayed in the myths of Isis and Osiris, of Shakti and Shiva, of Odin learning from Freyja, of Sophia among the Gnostics, Shekinah in the Jewish Kabbalah, of Demeter and the Mysteries of Eleusis. The Enki lineage of serpent wisdom, the knowledge of our cosmic origin and true genetic heritage, is demonized in the Bible, as already mentioned, and becomes an underground cultural stream of "Mystery Religion," as well as hermetic alchemy and astrology in Western civilization.

The mythology of rival brother extra-terrestrial gods is congruent with the evidence for two opposing forces or spirits guiding the human affairs at many levels. Seen more broadly, the descendants of the lineage of Enki as well as other deities (who may be ET races from other worlds) are creators, scientists, guides and teachers, who operate to provide guidance and technical assistance for humans wanting to realize their evolutionary potential and spiritual essence. The deities associated with the lineage of Enlil, which, according to some accounts, also including other visitor races from other worlds, are law-giving, rule-making dominators who established colonies on Earth for their own agendas, and continue to seek to exploit the resources of the planet and dominate the beings who they consider their domesticated worker-slaves. They dominate Earth beings using fear and threat, and the principle of "divide and conquer," and at times instigate religious wars among humans to consolidate their control agendas. They apparently regard humans, similarly to the way breeders of domestic animals might look after their herd, wanting to protect their investment.

It is interesting that scholars and writers who work on compiling and analyzing the huge numbers and variety of UFO/ET contact experiences, have similarly distinguished different groups of ET visitors, with diverse agendas (Salla, 2004; Horn, 1994; Bramley, 1989; Good, 1998; Mack, 1999). Some seem to have a beneficent and helpful purpose, providing knowledge and guidance to those humans with whom they interact, though adhering to a non-interference ethic on the global level; others have a more exploitative and controlling agenda, like animal breeders checking on their stock; yet others are apparently even more intrusive, harvesting the human genome for their own off-world purposes (these may be the ET visitors involved in the abduction scenarios studied by Harvard psychiatrist John Mack and others); yet others may be neutral, though interested, observers, like anthropologists observing an alien culture.

For myself, I don't feel a need to have a position on the presence or absence of UFO and ETs in our world of Earth

time and space. I find that to impartially consider and reflect
on the observations and stories reported by numerous credible
witnesses and scientists inevitably leads to a valuable expansion
of consciousness. It is this kind of expanded and deepened
awareness, and intelligent, critical reflection, not blind faith
and hope for escape, nor the fearful clinging to authoritative
opinions, that can ultimately have beneficial consequences for
us all. Given that disclaimer, I offer the following alternative and
complementary interpretations of the nature of extra-terrestrial or
inter-dimensional "alien" visitors (based on reports by various and
numerous observers):

1 – Some may be actual humanoid (two-legged, two-armed
form) visitors from other worlds, visiting Earth at the time-space
dimension, where they are perceived as aliens in UFOs, which
are space-faring vehicles clearly operating with technologies
as yet unknown by Earth scientists. (A sub-group of these are
sometimes reported to have features of reptiles, insects or birds;
most frequently they are reported to have huge black eyes and
grey skins).

2 – Human souls whose primary home is elsewhere in
our galaxy or beyond, who have taken human incarnation on
Earth (perhaps repeatedly), been conceived and born into a
human family and are indistinguishable in appearance from
humans indigenous to Earth. Such humans, sometimes called
"Wanderers," may develop conscious knowledge of their original
home and communicate, via "channeling" with their off-world
compatriots.

3 – A further variant, described by the medium Ruth
Montgomery as "walk-ins," are higher-dimensional beings
who have effected a kind of voluntary exchange with an adult
human personality, who then has access to vastly greater cosmic
knowledge and abilities. I have myself met at least one such self-

identified individual.

4 – Spirits with human-like souls from other worlds (who may or may not have incarnated previously on Earth) but now only "descend" as far as the intermediate frequency dimensions (mental-noetic, emotional-astral, perceptual-etheric), from where they communicate with human beings in visionary dreams or channelings, as "spirit guides." Some of these channeled extra-terrestrial guides and their present-day mediums give public talks, write books and have extensive human followers or students. With others there may be more or less unconscious guidance or suggestions that appear in dreams or other altered states. The council of malevolent dark force beings I encountered in the dream state, probably fall in this category.

5 – Highly advanced cosmic Beings of Light, whose true origin is in dimensions of reality that completely transcend our usual notions of planetary existence, who may be referred to as "angels," "deities," "devas" or "dakinis," who may have a light-energy form with humanoid outline (head, eyes, arms, wings), or spherical form, or be completely formless, and who communicate teachings or artistic/poetic inspiration through direct telepathic communion.

* * *

There are, indeed, "more things in the heavens and earth than are dreamed of in our philosophies," as the Bard said. In the next and concluding section of this essay, we will examine the astonishing record of the work of G.I. Gurdjieff, in which we find the themes of humanity's persistent compulsive war-making, and historical yet hidden interventions on Earth by higher-dimensional and extra-terrestrial beings, presented with fantastically elaborate complex detail and provocative insight.

G. I. Gurdjieff's Views on the Origins of War

One of the most remarkable spiritual teachers of the 20th century, G. I. Gurdjieff was born in the 1870s, in the Russian Caucasus region of mixed Greek and Armenian ancestry. This part of the world, at the gateway between Europe and Asia, was one where for hundreds of years, peoples of many different nationalities and languages migrated, co-existed and often fought. In his younger years he traveled extensively in Central Asia (including Tibet), and the Middle East (including Egypt). In his later years he lived in France, where he founded his Institute for the Harmonious Development of Man, and made several visits to America. Having experienced both Russian Revolutions, as well as both World Wars (he died in 1949), he certainly had ample opportunity to study the nature and origins of war and violence at first hand.

His teaching of practices of self-remembering and harmonious development, sometimes referred to as a Fourth Way teaching, was unique and original, although several writers have identified elements of Islamic Sufism, Greek and Russian Orthodox Christianity, Western esoteric, gnostic and hermetic traditions, as well as Buddhism and very ancient Asian, including Zoroastrian mystical traditions. In his writings and recorded talks, he himself stated repeatedly that his study of the causes of the "processes of reciprocal destruction" was one of the chief preoccupations of his life.

When Gurdjieff was living and teaching in Russia during the first decade of the 20th century, his talks were recorded in P.D. Ouspensky's *In Search of the Miraculous* (Ouspensky, 1949). Here, like the Buddhists, he emphasized the unconscious, sleep-like condition of ordinary human existence, captivated by external influences over which we had no control, and that we could only hope to awaken and free ourselves from these forces by deliberate and intentional practices of self-remembering, which is similar to the Buddhist emphasis on mindfulness. War, he said, was due to cosmic forces, or planetary influences. Just like when two people pass too near each other in the street causing momentary discomfort, two planets coming too near each in their orbits may result in tension, only momentary at the planetary scale – but on Earth, for a period of several years, "millions of sleeping men may start slaughtering other millions of sleeping men."

In his later years, when he was living and teaching in France, he wrote his *All and Everything – Beelzebub's Tales to his Grandson*, in which he expounded a much more involved and elaborate esoteric, historic, mythic tale, with his characteristic and undoubtedly intentional admixture of the fantastic, symbolic and obscure. His declared aim, in his writing, was not so much to inform or give opinions or theories, but to stimulate his readers to conscious intelligent thinking, and the development of what he called "objective conscience." With these reservations in mind, it is astonishing to note how much the stories that Gurdjieff unfolds, overlap with the esoteric histories that we have been discussing, and modern views from UFO/ET research.[7]

To begin with, the whole first volume (1200 pages long) of *All and Everything – Beelzebub's Tales to his Grandson –* is cast as an elaborate travel narrative, told on a spaceship, by the cosmic traveller Beelzebub (which is the name of a deity from Babylonian mythology) to his grandson Hassein. Beelzebub describes six "descents" he has made to the planet Earth, at different time periods in history, to different continents and countries, including

Atlantis, India, Tibet, and America; and describes at great length with many and elaborate complex details, using numerous neologisms seemingly pasted together from different languages, the characteristics, problems and possibilities of humans, or as he says, addressing Hassein, – "those three-brained beings that interest you so much." These six "descents" could be interpreted as meaning six human incarnations of a highly developed soul, on a quest for greater understanding of the human condition; or they could also be interpreted as actual descents in an actual space-ship, at different time periods, by visitors from another world, with a vastly advanced system of cosmic knowledge, making observations on planet Earth.

In the course of the narrative, Beelzebub–Gurdjieff refers repeatedly to certain "messengers sent from above," human incarnations of very high beings, who established religious teachings on Earth, including Moses, Jesus, Mohammed and especially a certain "Very Saintly Ashiata Shiemash," who taught on Earth during the ancient Sumero-Babylonian civilization (Shamash is also the name of a Sumerian deity). In addition to these, Beelzebub-Gurdjieff also refers, in his stories, to "Angels," "Archangels" and even a "High Commission" of "sacred beings," who are planetary engineers, physicists, and chemists, with whom he has conversations (i.e. or as we would say today, who he "channels"), and who have come to Earth at various times to address certain cosmic planetary problems that had arisen.

Chapter 43 of *Beelzebub's Tales to his Grandson*, entitled "Beelzebub's Survey of the Process of the Periodic Reciprocal Destruction of Men," opens with a passionate query from Hassein, who in trying to understand why humans, with their long history on the planet, and the fact that they have developed many systems of knowledge, still resort to wars: "Don't they really ever see that these processes of theirs are the most terrible of all the horrors which can possibly exist in the whole of the Universe and don't they ever ponder on this matter, so that they might become aware of this horror, and find a means of eradicating it?" In response to this question, Beelzebub then launches into a long discussion about the many attempts and agreements made by groups and leaders in various societies, throughout history, to investigate this process and to find ways to eradicate it – referring to the League of Nations as one of the most recent ones. He says that such groups, though usually starting with good intentions, have always tended to disintegrate into increasing divisiveness, as various leaders and groups participating in the discussions are taken over by egotism and greed, and end up instigating more war and destruction in order to profit from it for themselves and their group.

Beelzebub relates that "learned beings" in ancient times had discovered that there appeared to be some kind of natural planetary process, some kind of balancing process on a planetary scale, that constantly alternated periods of overpopulation of animals and humans, with periods of their destruction, regardless of what individuals wanted to do. Wars were totally unconscious, unintentional mass events, over which humans had no control. A key element in this cyclical situation was the human practice of dominating nature, that at times involved massive animal sacrifice, (and, one might add, human sacrifice, especially in ancient Meso-America). And Nature had to constantly adapt herself to these destructive practices of humans. This is an interesting adumbration of the ecological critique of the Judaeo-Christian domination of nature.

In this connection, Gurdjieff-Beelzebub then speaks of the

teachings of the "Very Saintly Ashiata Shiemash," a "Messenger sent from Above" during the Sumero-Babylonian civilization, who aimed at enhancing the development of objective consciousness and conscience in humans. These qualities of higher consciousness were to be developed through "conscious labor and intentional suffering." (This was also the guiding precept of the "work" that Gurdjieff taught at the Institute for the Harmonious Development of Man). The ordinary human condition, in which the development of objective consciousness was blocked, was due to the consequences of the "accursed organ *kundabuffer*." This organ, according to Beelzebub-Gurdjieff, had been implanted in human beings at the base of the spine, a very long time ago, by a group of "Very High, Very Sacred" angelic scientists, acting on instructions "from Above." Although the organ *kundabuffer* was subsequently removed, by other scientist angels, its operation had become crystallized and passed on genetically through the generations, to the point where it had become "second nature" in humans.

The maleficent residual consequences of this *kundabuffer* organ were that the psyche of humans is dominated by egotism, conceit, vanity, selfishness and the like, making it extremely difficult for them to develop objective consciousness and conscience, as well as making humans susceptible to being manipulated and exploited by leaders, war-mongers and ideologues for self-serving and profiteering motives. Although Beelzebub-Gurdjieff clearly considers the action and residual consequences of this implanted organ an unmitigated disaster for humans, he does report the results of his investigations and "conversations" with high angelic and archangelic beings as to the origins and intentions behind this genetic implant. Its origin had to do with certain cosmic planetary processes.

It appears that in very ancient times, even before the existence of the continent and civilization of Atlantis, there was a collision of a comet with planet Earth. This collision, Beelzebub avers, was due to "miscalculation" on the part of archangelic planetary engineers monitoring the intersecting orbits of cosmic bodies. It led to a crisis, because in accord with the basic cosmic laws of reciprocal maintenance, certain kinds of radiations and vibrational energies had to be produced on Earth. These kinds of energies could be produced by life, including human life, either consciously and qualitatively (as was done in certain temples in Atlantis) or unconsciously and quantitatively, through massive die-offs of human and animal populations (as has occurred in various planet-wide catastrophes, including floods, earthquakes, plagues and wars).

At the time of the original collision and the resulting threat to the maintenance of cosmic harmony in our planetary neighborhood, "a Most High Commission consisting of Angels and Archangels, specialists in the work of World Creation and World Maintenance," had "come down" from the Central Sun, and decided that this special organ *kundabuffer* needed to be installed in human beings. This organ was designed to prevent humans from developing objective consciousness, because if they did they would see the "terror of their situation," and "being convinced of their slavery to circumstances utterly foreign to them, they would be unwilling to continue their existence and would destroy themselves." So the *kundabuffer* that was installed had two functions: one, to cause human beings to "see reality upside down," and two, to engender in them sensations of pleasure and enjoyment. Some time after the immediate planetary crisis had passed, a further delegation of archangelic engineers and scientists caused the implant to be removed, but its consequences, as mentioned above, became crystallized and have remained part of the human genetic inheritance ever since.

Beelzebub-Gurdjieff does not further explain how exactly the functioning of the organ kundabuffer, originally designed to prevent a kind of traumatic suicide reaction on the part of humans, then led to the maleficent congenital features we have been laboring under ever since. One could perhaps think of the connection this way: "seeing reality upside-down" is a kind of perceptual inversion, causing humans to fixate only on the physical plane as real, and ignore the greater realities accessible to objective consciousness, where they would have clearly seen their enslaved condition, and therefore the "terror of their situation." Furthermore, the enhanced capacities for pleasure and enjoyment provided a kind of tranquilizing balm, which then manifested as the addictive over development of craving that we know as egotism, vanity, conceit, self-importance, greed and the like. This view is reminiscent of the Buddha's analysis of the human condition, which regards unconscious cravings in the material realm as the root cause of our suffering. Although the original planetary collision crisis which led to the implantation of this perceptual block has long passed, the need for human life on Earth to contribute certain energies for harmonious cosmic functioning remains – and if not provided by the intentional conscious spiritual work of humans, these energies are generated automatically by massive population increases and consequent massive die-offs due to natural catastrophes and war.

Gurdjieff, speaking as the space-travelling narrator

Beelzebub, as well as quoting his spiritual ancestor the "Very Saintly Ashiata Shiemash," provides two separate rather sobering and mysterious answers to the question of whether war can be eradicated and humans can be saved. At the end of the long chapter on "the processes of periodic reciprocal destruction," Beelzebub concludes that "if this property of terrestrial beings is to disappear from that unfortunate planet, then it will be with Time alone, thanks either to the guidance of a certain Being with very high Reason or to certain cosmic events."

At the very end of *Beelzebub's Tales to his Grandson*, after more than a thousand pages of these extraordinary ruminations and explications, Hassein asks his teacher-grandfather again to state, in a summary way, from "your long-centuried impartial observations and studies of the psyche of the three-centered beings arising on the planet Earth…whether it is still possible by some means or other to save them and to direct them into the becoming path?" Beelzebub then, with great emphasis, replies: "The sole means now for the saving of the beings of the planet Earth would be to implant again into their presences a new organ, an organ like *kundabuffer*, but this time of such properties that everyone of these unfortunates during the process of existence should constantly sense and be cognizant of the inevitability of his own death as well as the death of everyone upon whom his eyes or attention rests." (Gurdjieff, 1950, p. 1183)[8]

These two answers reflect a conviction that the underlying causes of war are cosmic-planetary in nature, of which humans are more or less completely unconscious, and over which they have very little or no control. It is possible, but difficult, for individuals to undergo transformations of their psyche, through "conscious labor and intentional suffering," and, one might add, through psychospiritual yogic and mystical practices, by which they can awaken to their spiritual essence and liberate themselves from the thralldom of unconsciousness. In my own comparative studies of transformative experiences, described in the book *The Unfolding Self* (Metzner, 1998), I found that the catalyst for the most profound life-changing and worldview-changing turning-points was coming close to confronting one's own mortality, either through near-death experiences (NDEs), or through the death of a loved one. The death-rebirth Mystery ritual celebrations of ancient times, as well as certain shamanic initiations may have provided this kind of awakening. Psychedelic experiences can also provide this kind of insight and awakening, given the appropriate preparation and guidance.

While the individual awakening of consciousness is possible and is certainly our primary responsibility, the transformation of collective consciousness from the bondage created by unconscious cravings and hatreds, in a situation of rapidly deteriorating planetary environments and the slow-motion collapse of civilization, would seem to be an extremely difficult, if not totally impossible challenge. It is in this sense that I would understand Gurdjieff–Beelzebub's seemingly bizarre and improbable prescription.

Concluding Reflections

There are many themes in this story reminiscent of various Gnostic teachings, according to which Earth has been subject to mistakes and miscalculations on the part of a creator demiurge. Gurdjieff's story also has parallels in Sumerian mythology, as interpreted by Sitchin – not surprising since Gurdjieff himself implicitly refers to his spiritual ancestry in the Sumero-Babylonian civilization. The most striking parallel is in the teachings that humans have been intentionally and deliberately kept in a subservient, slave-like condition by their superiors, to provide certain kinds of energies (whether for mining work or planetary maintenance).

The biggest difference between the two accounts is that Sitchin's reading of the activities of the Annunaki and their Mesopotamian human underlings is purely concerned with the material level – the "gods" are nothing but long-lived ETs flying around in space-ships. Gurdjieff's cosmology, on the other hand, reflects the multidimensional nature of cosmic reality and human consciousness, and the "descent" of divine beings and human interactions with them are as much interdimensional as interplanetary events. Other writers on the role of extra-terrestrial interventions in human history and civilization, including William Bramley and Arthur David Horn, have also supposed that deliberate conditioning processes on the part of dominator elites have kept the human workers and slaves unconscious of their inherent but undeveloped spiritual essence and potential autonomy.

Of great interest for me personally, in the light of my research in the psychological aspects of the planetary ecological crisis, is the prescient foreshadowing in this story, of the manner in which the destructive industrial activities of humans, and the reckless pursuit of power and profit, leads to increasingly disastrous consequences for the natural balance of the Gaian biosphere. Indigenous elders, such as the Hopis in the American Southwest and many others, have been warning us in their prophecies for a long time that the balancing adaptations of Nature to the seemingly unconscious, yet also deliberate destructive and exploitative behavior of humans are manifesting, and will be manifesting, in potentially near-total collapse of our planetary civilization.

A distinctive feature of Gurdjieff's reading of the hidden historic and pre-historic antecedents of war, is that it goes deeper than the simplistic dualisms of good versus evil, or light versus dark forces, pervasive throughout ancient religious mythology and occult histories, as well as much of the UFO/ET literature of modern times. In Gurdjieff's view, as in Buddhism, the wars and destructiveness, the domination and victimization behaviors of human beings, are the result of unconscious psychic factors in them that block awareness of their spiritual essence, or as the Buddhist say, their inherent "Buddha nature." And those root unconscious blocking factors were not installed by dominator spirits seeking to enslave us (although such beings may exist at some level), but rather they were the unintended malignant consequences of measures that were taken, by very high supra-dimensional cosmic beings, to stabilize orbital planetary perturbations and ameliorate the potential shock to humans when they would become aware of the dangerous conditions of existence intrinsic to living on planet Earth.

Since Gurdjieff was in the habit of concealing nuggets of

information in his neologisms, various readers of his books have speculated on the derivation of the word *kundabuffer*. One obvious possibility, suggested also by the location of the organ at the base of the spine, is that it refers to a buffer of kundalini energy, which lies coiled at the root chakra at the base of the spine. According to traditional Indian yoga teachings, when the kundalini energy is awakened and connects with the crown chakra, a state of cosmic consciousness can be attained. Gurdjieff himself, in his earlier teachings as recorded by Ouspensky, states however that the kundalini process is completely misunderstood, and in modern times is associated with nothing but fantasy and imagination.

For me, this speculative etymology of the meaning of *kundabuffer* relates to a somewhat different reading of mankind's esoteric antecedents that I heard from my teacher of Agni Yoga, an American clairvoyant healer-teacher named Russell Schofield, who died in 1984. Though it was not the main focus of his teaching, which was healing through body-centered light-fire energy work, Schofield did at times make some statements derived from his reading of the *akashic record* – during a time when he and I were collaborating on an unfinished and unpublished writing project. The *akashic record* is considered to be the knowledge repository of all past events, at every level of all dimensions, on all planets and everywhere in the Universe. As I have come to understand it, at a certain level of psychospiritual advancement these records can be selectively accessed, when one's spiritual purpose calls for bringing through that knowledge. An example was the noted American psychic Edgar Cayce who, while in a sleep-state, accessed knowledge of ancient civilizations like Egypt and Atlantis, in the context of providing healing information for people who consulted him.

Since there is no way to independently verify statements derived from such a source, I present these views, and those of Gurdjieff, not as "true" in any ordinary sense, but rather as offering "food for thought" and perspectives that can lead to further questioning and searching.

Schofield related that a block or seal was implanted on the generative or "root" energy-center, by the high-level cosmic light-beings and adepts who are guiding human evolution, after the collapse of the continent of Atlantis – because of the misuse of that energy by certain leaders of the Atlantean civilization (misuse that Cayce also spoke about at length). The serpentine generative energy, also called kundalini, whose source is at the sacral root-center, in ordinary human life generates the biological life-force for building cells and maintaining the vitality of the organism (one band of this energy spectrum providing the energy of procreative sex). This energy was used by those Atlantean initiates who were on a dark power path, to create living human-animal hybrids as worker-slaves (as Edgar Cayce had also reported), as well as some insects and microbes as biological weaponry for their domination agendas.

As a result of this misuse of the generative energy, and to prevent it from recurring, the possibility of actually creating living biological forms was sealed off for humans, and the expression of creative power limited to the mental level only. We can create systems of ideas, designs and images, and give them form in buildings, paintings, music, literature, sculpture, music and all the other forms of art and invention – but we cannot create living biological entities. The process of implantation of this seal in successive human generations presumably took some time, and involved also the collaboration of advanced human initiates, including the Hebrew adept King Solomon. The esoteric sigil design known as Solomon's Seal is said to be an emblem of his participation in this process. (Solomon's involvement in the *kundabuffer* story is also mentioned by Gurdjieff, but with a different twist).

To *summarize*, I have presented two variants of an esoteric teaching regarding an implant in the human energy system that has functioned, and still functions, as a block on the evolution of higher consciousness and a consequent inability to transcend destructive and divisive tendencies inherent in the human condition. In one version, the block was implanted to prevent and forestall further misuse of higher-frequency energies for power and domination agendas. In the other version, the block was implanted for temporary reasons of cosmic necessity and human welfare, but had the unintended negative consequences of fixating human awareness and striving on the material level of consciousness (or unconsciousness).

Unconsciousness *(avidya)* or forgetfulness, combined with cravings and hatreds, is the basic human condition of both dominators and slaves, predators and prey, soldiers and traders, the powerful and the poor. That is the curse and the poison of human existence on planet Earth. However, teachers and teachings have appeared, and continue to appear, to show the pathways to remembrance and liberation. New generations of children continue to be born, their innocence intact, into fortunate circumstances of family and community, where the awareness of their spiritual essence can be nurtured and supported. That is the mercy and the blessing, and the precious opportunity of human life.

Notes

[1] *Meme*, coined by analogy with 'gene,' by Richard Dawkins, is an idea considered as a replicator, especially with the connotation that memes parasitize people into propagating them much as viruses do.

[2] Describing his forthcoming book *The Origins of War in the Child Abuse*, De Mause writes: "This book is based on the premise that the evolution of amounts of interpersonal violence, terrorism and war is dependent upon the evolution of historical personality types, which I call "psychoclasses." This evolution, in turn, depends upon the historical evolution of childrearing modes. The evidence for the evolution of childrearing has been the subject of seven books and over eighty scholarly articles by myself published during the past four decades, backed up by the findings of over fifty psychohistorical colleagues which I have published in my scholarly journals, *The Journal of Psychohistory* and *The Journal of Psychoanalytic Anthropology.*

The evolution of childrearing is an uneven historical process, both within societies and in different areas of the world, so each nation today has all six personality modes, or "psychoclasses," within it, forming its various levels of political behavior from reactionary to progressive. Nevertheless, the evolution of childrearing modes and historical personalities – which I term "psychogenesis" – has improved personalities over the centuries in almost all areas of the globe, reducing the violence produced by abusive and abandoning parenting.

The infanticide, tying up, starving, battering, torture and rape of children that has been routine in history will be examined in more detail in later chapters of this book. Even today, however, most children in most nations are badly abused and neglected in their early years. This is denied by most people. A recent survey by British doctors, for instance, said they believed the child sexual abuse rate was "probably less than one percent," while careful studies of U.K. childhood sexual assault showed two-thirds of girls and one-third of boys had been used sexually. The figures for the U.S. are about the same. Figures for less advanced societies are even higher, where, for instance, many Islamic societies still raping the majority of both girls and boys, and "infanticide, abandonment of babies, to beating, shaking, burning, cutting, poisoning" are found to be common. Since Islamic females traditionally have had their genitals painfully cut off as young girls (in Egypt today, for instance, 97 percent of uneducated families and 66 percent of educated families still practice female genital mutilation), it is hard to be surprised that they grow up to be less than effective mothers. (DeMause, 2007b).

[3] Most mothers in history and a majority of mothers even today experience post-partum depression, which badly affects their ability to take care of and show love and empathy for their babies. It is bad enough that child care is itself so demanding…studies that show that 80% of mothers experience either (1) mild "baby blues" for months after birth, (2) post-partum depression for up to seven years, or (3) puerperal psychosis: "They feel low, anxious, tearful,

and irritable. They have rapid mood swings…feel hopeless…experience panic attacks…feel worthless, inadequate…have suicidal thoughts and thoughts of harming or killing their children." (DeMause, Lloyd, 2007a)

[4] Sapolsky relates the story of how a tuberculosis epidemic that devastated two neighboring and competing troops of savanna baboons, created a kind of "selective bottleneck," in which the most aggressive males died, leaving more affiliative ones, and skewing the female to male ratio. "The social consequences of these changes were dramatic. There remained a hierarchy, but it was far looser than before: …high-ranking males rarely harassed subordinates and occasionally even relinquished contested resources to them. Aggression was less frequent, particularly against third parties. And rates of affiliative behaviors, such as males and females grooming each other or sitting together, soared. There were even instances, now and then, of adult males grooming each other – a behavior nearly as unprecedented as baboons sprouting wings. … But the largest surprise did not come until some years later. …By the early 1990s, none of the original low aggression/high affiliation males of Forest Troop's tuberculosis period was still alive; all of the group's adult males had joined after the epidemic. Despite this, the troop's unique milieu persisted – at it does to this day, some 20 years after the selective bottleneck. In other words, adolescent males that enter Forest Troop after having grown up elsewhere wind up adopting the unique behavioral style of the resident males. As defined by both anthropologists and animal behaviorists, "culture" consists of local behavioral variations, occurring for nongenetic and nonecological reasons that last beyond the time of their originators. Forest Troop's low aggression/high affiliation society constitutes nothing less than a multigenerational benign culture (Sapolsky, 2006).

[5] The non-military functions of the war system that the *Report* identifies are:

- *Economic:* War has provided both ancient and modern societies with a dependable system of stabilizing and controlling national economies.

- *Political:* The permanent possibility of war is the foundation of stable government; it supplies the basis for general acceptance of political authority …has ensured the subordination of the citizen to the state, by virtue of the residual war powers inherent in the concept of nationhood.

- *Sociological:* War has uniquely served societies, throughout history, as an indispensable controller of dangerous social dissidence and destructive antisocial tendencies…The war system has provided the machinery through which the motivational forces governing human behavior have been translated into binding social allegiance. .. and thus ensured the degree of social cohesion necessary to the viability of nations.

- *Ecological:* War has been the principal evolutionary device for maintaining a satisfactory ecological balance between gross human population and supplies available for its survival.

- *Cultural and Scientific:* In modern societies, the development of the arts and sciences .. has been corollary to the parallel development of weaponry. (From: *Report from Iron Mountain, pp 80-82*).

[6] *The Project for a New American Century* (PNAC) and its policy statements is one of the expressions of a loose association variously referred to as the "Global Dominance Group" or the "Higher-Circle Policy Elite," that emerged in the US during the Reagan years and the second Bush regime. For a detailed discussion of these groups and identifications of their most significant players, see the volume *9/11 and the American Empire*, edited by David Ray Griffin and Peter Dale Scott, especially the chapter on "Parameters of Power in the Global Dominance Group," by Peter Phillips and his associates (pp 169-188).

[7] One of the most detailed and scientifically sophisticated ET contact experiences is recorded by Elizabeth Klarer, in her 1980 book *Beyond the Light Barrier*, which is currently out-of-print (http://beyondthelightbarrier.com). Her alien visitor contacts related geophysical and social turmoil on Earth to cyclical increases in the intensity of solar flare eruptions.

[8] Gurdjieff-Beelzebub continues: "Only such a sensation and such cognizance can now destroy the egoism completely crystallized in them that has swallowed up the whole of their Essence and also that tendency to hate others which flows from it – the tendency, namely, which engenders all those mutual relationships existing there, which serve as the chief cause of all their abnormalities unbecoming to three-brained beings and maleficent for them themselves and for the whole of the Universe." (*op.cit.*, p. 1183)

References

Anonymous. *Report form Iron Mountain.* (with Introduction by Lenard C. Lewin) NY: Dial Press, 1967.

Andreas, Joel. *Addicted to War. Why the US Can't Kick Militarism.* Oakland, CA: AK Press, 2002.

Blum, William. *Rogue State – A Guide to the World's Only Superpower.* Monroe, ME: Common Courage Press, 2000.

Bramley, William. *The Gods of Eden.* N.Y: Avon Books, 1989.

DeMause, Lloyd. *The Foundations of Psychohistory.* N.Y: Creative Roots, Inc. 1982.

DeMause, Lloyd. "The Killer Motherland" in *Journal of Psychohistory,* 34 (4), Spring 2007a.

DeMause, Lloyd. "The Psychology and Neurobiology of Violence." in *Journal of Psychohistory.* 35 (2), Fall 2007b.

DeWaal, Frans and Lanting, Frans. *Bonobo – The Forgotten Ape.* University of California Press, 1997.

Gimbutas, Marija. *The Civilization of the Goddess.* San Francisco: Harper Collins, 1991.

Grof, Stanislav. *Realms of the Human Unconscious.* N.Y: E.P. Dutton, 1976.

Grof, Stanislav. *Psychology of the Future – Lessons from Modern Consciousness Research.* Albany, NY: SUNY Press, 2000.

Gurdjieff, G.I. *All and Everything – Beelzebub's Tales to his Grandson.* New York: E.P. Dutton, 1950.

Hope, Murry. *Atlantis – Myth or Reality?* London: Arkana Penguin Books, 1991.

Horn, Arthur David. *Humanity's Extra-Terrestrial Origins.* Lake Montezuma, AZ: A & L Horn, 1994.

Jenkins, John Major. *Galactic Alignment.* Rochester, VT: Bear & Co., 2002.

Klein, Naomi. *The Shock Doctrine: The Rise of Disaster Capitalism.* London: Metropolitan Books, 2007

Lovelock, James. *Healing Gaia: Practical Medicine for the Planet.* New York: Harmony Books, 1991.

Magdoff, Harry. *Imperialism.* NY: Monthly Review Press, 1978.

Metzner, Ralph. *The Unfolding Self -Varieties of Transformative Experience.* Novato: Origin Press, 1998.

Metzner, Ralph. *The Well of Remembrance*. Boston: Shambhala, 1994.

Metzner, Ralph. "The Buddhist Six-Worlds Model of Consciousness and Reality." *Journal of Transpersonal Psychology*, 1996, Vol. 28, No. 2.

Ouspensky, P. D. *In Search of the Miraculous*. NY: Harcourt, Brace and World, 1949.

Salla, Michael. *Exopolitics: Political Implications of Extraterrestrial Presence*. Tempe, AZ: Dandelion Books, 2004.

Schellhorn, G. Cope. *Extraterrestrials in Biblical Prophecy*. Madison, WI: Horus House Press, 1989.

Schmookler, Andrew Bard. T*he Parable of the Tribes*. Berkeley: University of California Press, 1984.

Shepard, Paul. *Thinking Animals: Animals and the Development of Human Intelligence*. New York: Viking Press, 1978.

Shiva, Vandana. S*tolen Harvest – The Hijacking of the Global Food Supply*. Cambridge, MA: South End Press, 2000.

Sitchin, Zachariah. *The Twelfth Planet*. N.Y: Avon Books, 1976.

Sitchin, Zachariah. *The Wars of Gods and Men*. N.Y.: Avon Books, 1985

Sitchin, Zachariah. *Genesis Revisited*. N.Y.; Avon Books, 1990.

Shepard, Paul. *Thinking Animals*. N.Y.: Viking Press, 1978.

Shepard, Paul. *Nature and Madness*. San Francisco: Sierra Club Books, 1982.

Snyder, Gary. *The Practice of the Wild*. San Francisco: Northpoint Press, 1990.

Steiner, Rudolf. *Secret Brotherhoods and the Mystery of the Human Double* (1917 Lectures) Rudolf Steiner Press, 2004.

Webre, Alfred. *Exopolitics: Politics, Government, and Law in the Universe*. Vancouver: Universebooks, 2000.

Green Earth Foundation
Harmonizing Humanity with Earth and Spirit

The Green Earth Foundation is an educational and research organization dedicated to the healing and harmonizing of the relationships between humanity and the Earth, through a recognition of the energetic and spiritual interconnectedness of all life-forms in all worlds. Our strategic objectives are to help bring about changes in attitudes, values, perceptions, and worldviews that are based on ecological balance and respect for the integrity of all life. Our areas of research interest include consciousness studies, shamanism and Earth mythology, and green and eco-psychology. Green Earth Foundation also sponsors the *Metzner Alchemical Divination*® training program.

Green Earth Founation
is producing and co-publishing a new series of books
by Ralph Metzner, Ph.D. –

THE ECOLOGY OF CONSCIOUSNESS

1. The Expansion of Consciousness

2. The Roots of War and Domination

3. Varieties of States of Consciousness

4. Alchemical Divination

5. The Psychology of Incarnation, Birth and Death

6. Worlds Within and Worlds Beyond

The Green Earth Foundation is a 501(c)(3) non-profit, educational and research organization. P.O. Box 327, El Verano. CA 95433. Internet: www.greenearthfound.org

Alchemical Divination

Alchemy is the ancient art and science of elemental transformation. The focus of alchemical practicioners was healing and what we would nowadays call psychotherapy, as well as spiritual growth and understanding. *Alchemy*, like shamanism and yoga, with which it is related, involves teachings and practices of physical, psychic and spiritual transformation, expressed in the imaginal language of material transformation.

Divination is the practice of seeking healing, insight and guidance from inner sources commonly called the "spirit world" or "divine world", or one's intuition or Higher Self. We are most familiar with divination accessories or tools such as the Tarot, the I Ching, or the Nordic Runes; but the essence of the process is the asking of questions and receiving answers from inner sources of knowledge and guidance.

The *alchemical divinations* developed by Ralph Metzner are processes of structured intuitive inquiry, using light-fire yoga methods for a heightened state of concentrative awareness. We work in the spirit of the Roman deity Janus, god of doorways, passages and transitions, whose two faces look in a balanced way into the past and the future.

The basic purpose of these alchemical divinations is to help individuals obtain deeper experiential understanding, problem resolution and visionary inspiration for their life path in its intrapsychic, interpersonal, professional, creative and spiritual dimensions.

The *Metzner Alchemical Divination*® training program consists of three, modular 5-day workshops, taught in the US and in Europe, in which one learns the divinations for oneself, and how to conduct them for others.

Please consult the website: www.metzneralchemicaldivination.org, for details.

Metzner Alchemical Divination® is a registered trademark.